**Communications
in Computer and Information Science**   2734

Series Editors

Gang Li, *School of Information Technology, Deakin University, Burwood, VIC,
Australia*
Joaquim Filipe, *Polytechnic Institute of Setúbal, Setúbal, Portugal*
Zhiwei Xu, *Chinese Academy of Sciences, Beijing, China*

Rationale

The CCIS series is devoted to the publication of proceedings of computer science conferences. Its aim is to efficiently disseminate original research results in informatics in printed and electronic form. While the focus is on publication of peer-reviewed full papers presenting mature work, inclusion of reviewed short papers reporting on work in progress is welcome, too. Besides globally relevant meetings with internationally representative program committees guaranteeing a strict peer-reviewing and paper selection process, conferences run by societies or of high regional or national relevance are also considered for publication.

Topics

The topical scope of CCIS spans the entire spectrum of informatics ranging from foundational topics in the theory of computing to information and communications science and technology and a broad variety of interdisciplinary application fields.

Information for Volume Editors and Authors

Publication in CCIS is free of charge. No royalties are paid, however, we offer registered conference participants temporary free access to the online version of the conference proceedings on SpringerLink (http://link.springer.com) by means of an http referrer from the conference website and/or a number of complimentary printed copies, as specified in the official acceptance email of the event.

CCIS proceedings can be published in time for distribution at conferences or as post-proceedings, and delivered in the form of printed books and/or electronically as USBs and/or e-content licenses for accessing proceedings at SpringerLink. Furthermore, CCIS proceedings are included in the CCIS electronic book series hosted in the SpringerLink digital library at http://link.springer.com/bookseries/7899. Conferences publishing in CCIS are allowed to use our online conference service (Meteor) for managing the whole proceedings lifecycle (from submission and reviewing to preparing for publication) free of charge.

Publication process

The language of publication is exclusively English. Authors publishing in CCIS have to sign the Springer CCIS copyright transfer form, however, they are free to use their material published in CCIS for substantially changed, more elaborate subsequent publications elsewhere. For the preparation of the camera-ready papers/files, authors have to strictly adhere to the Springer CCIS Authors' Instructions and are strongly encouraged to use the CCIS LaTeX style files or templates.

Abstracting/Indexing

CCIS is abstracted/indexed in DBLP, Google Scholar, EI-Compendex, Mathematical Reviews, SCImago, Scopus. CCIS volumes are also submitted for the inclusion in ISI Proceedings.

How to start

To start the evaluation of your proposal for inclusion in the CCIS series, please send an e-mail to ccis@springer.com

Alan Talevi · Vinicius Rosa Cota

Editors

Computational Neuroscience

5th Latin American Workshop, LAWCN 2025
La Plata, Argentina, November 12–14, 2025
Revised Selected Papers

 Springer

Editors
Alan Talevi ⓘD
National University of La Plata
La Plata, Argentina

Vinicius Rosa Cota ⓘD
Maynooth University
Maynooth, Ireland

ISSN 1865-0929 ISSN 1865-0937 (electronic)
Communications in Computer and Information Science
ISBN 978-3-032-14663-2 ISBN 978-3-032-14664-9 (eBook)
https://doi.org/10.1007/978-3-032-14664-9

This Springer imprint is published by the registered company Springer Nature Switzerland AG
The registered company address is: Gewerbestrasse 11, 6330 Cham, Switzerland

If disposing of this product, please recycle the paper.

Preface

The Latin American Workshop on Computational Neurosciences (LAWCN) is a regional biennial event that promotes the dissemination of recent findings and ideas in the field of neuroscience—particularly at its intersections with computer science, engineering, and artificial intelligence—within the Latin American community, and with an international outlook.

The fifth edition of the workshop (LAWCN 2025) was held in the city of La Plata, Argentina, the first fully planned and designed city in Latin America and one of the earliest examples of modern urban planning in the world, from November 12–14, 2025. All manuscripts included in this volume were reviewed by at least two experienced reviewers from our Scientific Committee in an open-review process. Ten out of a total of twelve submitted papers were accepted. While highly interdisciplinary in nature, they have been grouped under the areas of artificial intelligence and machine learning, neuroengineering, and computational neuroscience.

LAWCN 2025 was organized by the Laboratory of Bioactive Compound Research and Development (LIDeB) of the National University of La Plata (UNLP), the third oldest university in Argentina. UNLP is often ranked the second or third most important university in the country and among the top twenty on the continent.

The conference was endorsed by several national and international organizations, including the Federation of Latin American and Caribbean Neuroscience Societies, the Colombian College of Neuroscience (COLNE), CINVESTAV Sede Sur, Potsdam University, LATBrain, Federal University of São João del-Rei, ApoyoDravet, and the International Research Network on Dravet and Refractory Epilepsy (INDRE), and generously sponsored by Fundación Ciencias Exactas, the International Brain Research Organization, Plexon, Boolzi, and eLife. Finally, Springer Nature has become a key collaborator of LAWCN as the publisher of our top papers in the very reputable book series CCIS. We are thankful to this publishing house and to the CCIS staff.

We would like to express our gratitude to these organizations, the keynote speakers, the authors, and all the participants for helping us put together an awesome event and this excellent book.

October 2025

Alan Talevi
Vinicius Rosa Cota

Organization

General Chairs

Alan Talevi   National University of La Plata, Argentina
Vinicius Rosa Cota   Maynooth University, Ireland

Program Committee Chairs

Alan Talevi   National University of La Plata, Argentina
Vinicius Rosa Cota   Maynooth University, Ireland

Steering Committee

Lucas Alberca	National University of La Plata, Argentina
Lina Becerra Hernández	Universidad del Valle & Universidad Pontificia Javeriana, Colombia
Emilia Barrionuevo	National University of La Plata, Argentina
Carolina Bellera	National University of La Plata, Argentina
Virginia Chaulet	National University of La Plata, Argentina
Dante Augusto Couto Barone	Federal University of Rio Grande do Sul, Brazil
Maximiliano Fallico	National University of La Plata, Argentina
Melisa Gantner	National University of La Plata, Argentina
Norberto Garcìa Cairasco	University of São Paulo, Brazil
Luciana Gavernet	National University of La Plata, Argentina
Giuliana Muraca	National University of La Plata, Argentina
Estefanía Peralta	National University of La Plata, Argentina
Victoria Peterson	National University of the Littoral, Argentina
Denis Prada Gori	National University of La Plata, Argentina
Jaime Riascos Salas	Potsdam University, Germany & Institución Universitaria de Envigado, Brazil
Luisa Rocha Arrieta	Centro de Investigación y de Estudios Avanzados del Instituto Politécnico Nacional, Mexico
Santiago Ruatta	National University of La Plata, Argentina
María Esperanza Ruiz	National University of La Plata, Argentina
Sebastián Scioli Montoto	National University of La Plata, Argentina

Program Committee

Lucas Alberca	National University of La Plata, Argentina
Romis Attux	University of Campinas, Brazil
Lina Becerra Hernández	Universidad del Valle & Universidad Pontificia Javeriana, Colombia
Carolina Bellera	National University of La Plata. Argentina
Omar Carmona Cortes	Instituto Federal do Maranhão, Brazil
Gabriela Castellano	University of Campinas, Brazil
Michela Chiappalone	University of Genoa, Italy
Josenildo Costa da Silva	Instituto Federal do Maranhão, Brazil
Dante Couto Barone	Federal University of Rio Grande do Sul, Brazil
Antônio da Silva Filho	University of São Paulo, Brazil
Paulo Rogério de Almeida Ribeiro	Federal University of Maranhão, Brazil
Harlei Miguel de Arruda Leite	Aeronautics Institute of Technology, Brazil
Edison Pignaton de Freitas	Federal University of Rio Grande do Sul, Brazil
Flávio Afonso Gonçalves Mourão	University of Illinois Urbana-Champaign, USA
Dimitris Kugiumtzis	University of Thessaloniki, Greece
Carlos Dias Maciel	University of São Paulo, Brazil
Jean Faber Ferreira de Abreu	Federal University of São Paulo, Brazil
Melisa Gantner	National University of La Plata, Argentina
Luciana Gavernet	National University of La Plata, Argentina
Daniel Lima Gomes Júnior	Instituto Federal do Maranhão, Brazil
Dania Gutiérrez	Centro de Investigación y de Estudios Avanzados, Mexico
Manuel Llanos	Scripps Research, USA
Juan Francisco Morales	University of Florida, USA
Patricio Orio	University of Valparaíso, Chile
Marcelo Pias	Federal University of Rio Grande, Brazil
Nivaldo Portela de Vasconcelos	Federal University of Pernambuco, Brazil
Jaime Riascos Salas	Potsdam University, Germany & Institución Universitaria de Envigado, Brazil
Vinicius Rosa Cota	Maynooth University, Ireland
Alan Talevi	National University of La Plata, Argentina
Julian Tejada	University of Sergipe, Brazil
Jim Tørresen	University of Oslo, Norway

Additional Reviewers

Vinicius Maltarollo	Federal University of Minas Gerais, Brazil

Contents

Artificial Intelligence and Machine Learning

Multimodal Physiological Signal Statistical Analysis and Random Forest Classification for Epileptic Seizure Detection

Adrian Montes-Chirito[1], Corina Flores-Ochoa[2], Grace Inga-Quispe[3], and Erick Toque[1]([✉])

[1] Pontificia Universidad Católica del Perú, Av. Universitaria 1801, San Miguel, 15088 Lima, Peru
`ericktoque22@gmail.com`
[2] Universidad Nacional Autónoma de Honduras, Boulevard Suyapa, Tegucigalpa 11101, Honduras
[3] Universidad de Ingeniería y Tecnología, Jr. Medrano Silva 165, Barranco, 15063 Lima, Peru

Abstract. Epilepsy faces diagnostic challenges due to the low sensitivity of scalp EEG and the subjectivity of its manual interpretation. This study analyzes multimodal physiological signals (EEG, ECG, EMG, and ACC/GYR) using statistical methods to identify features that can reliably discriminate between ictal and non-ictal events. Descriptive analysis, significance tests (Mann-Whitney U, Cliff's Delta), and inter-signal correlation analyses were applied to extract interpretable and physiologically metrics. Additionally, these features were used to train a Random Forest classifier, achieving promising results across EEG, ECG, and EMG modalities (F1-score:0.79, 0.77, and 0.75 respectively). The model's performance demonstrates that metrics such as amplitude range and standard deviation, selected through prior statistical analysis, provide sufficient discriminative power for automatic seizure detection. These findings highlight the importance of interpretable signal features as a foundation for explainable machine learning systems in clinical and portable contexts.

Keywords: Statistical analysis · Machine learning · Epilepsy · Interpretability · Physiological signals

1 Introduction

Epilepsy is one of the most prevalent neurological disorders worldwide, affecting over 50 million individuals [1]. It is characterized by recurrent seizures resulting from abnormal, excessive, or synchronous neuronal activity [2]. Although pharmacological and surgical treatments exist, approximately 30% of patients suffer from drug-resistant epilepsy (DRE) [3]. Electroencephalography (EEG) is the standard tool for recording cerebral electrical activity during ictal episodes

© The Author(s), under exclusive license to Springer Nature Switzerland AG 2026
A. Talevi and V. Rosa Cota (Eds.): LAWCN 2025, CCIS 2734, pp. 3–11, 2026.
https://doi.org/10.1007/978-3-032-14664-9_1

[4]. However, its diagnostic sensitivity ranges between 29% and 55% [5], and its interpretation relies on manual assessment by specialists, leading to moderate inter-rater agreement (kappa index = 0.50) [6].

In response to these limitations, multisensory wearable devices have been developed, integrating EEG with additional physiological signals to enhance diagnostic precision [7]. Among these, electrocardiography (ECG) detects heart rate alterations during seizures [8]; electromyography (EMG) captures abnormal muscle activity in motor events [9]; and accelerometry and gyroscope sensors (ACC/GYR) track characteristic seizure-related movements [7]. These complementary signals enable a more comprehensive characterization of the patient's physiological state before, during, and after seizures, thus increasing diagnostic potential [10].

In this context, the large volume and complexity of data generated by wearable systems make epileptic seizure detection an ideal challenge for data science methodologies. Statistical methods play a central role by facilitating the identification of relevant patterns through descriptive metrics such as mean, standard deviation, and amplitude range [11], along with non-parametric inference techniques like the Mann–Whitney U test and effect size estimators such as Cliff's Delta [12,13]. Additionally, Pearson correlation matrices are used to examine intermodal interactions and capture the coupling between signals under different physiological states [14].

This work seeks to establish a methodological framework for the automatic detection of epileptic seizures. The central aim of this study is to demonstrate that a feature set, derived from multimodal physiological signals and refined through statistical analysis, can serve as input for a high-performance Random Forest classifier.

2   Methodology

This study applies a data science approach to explore physiological differences between ictal and non-ictal states using multimodal biosignals. It combines classical statistical analysis with computational techniques such as SMOTE and Random Forest. As a proof of concept, a Random Forest classifier is used due to its robustness to noise, ability to handle multiple variables, and interpretability [15,16]. The dataset used is the SeizeIT2 multicenter database, developed by KU Leuven, Belgium [17]. All analyses were conducted on anonymized data under ethical approval (ID: S63631; amendment S67350) (Fig. 1).

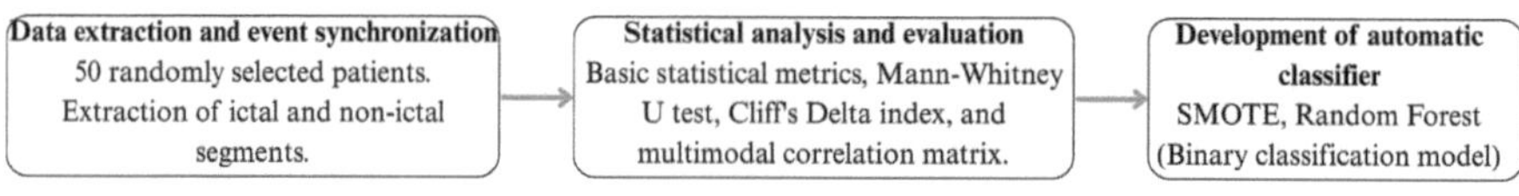

Fig. 1. Flowchart of the methodology for epileptic seizure detection.

2.1 Data Extraction and Synchronization

Physiological recordings were obtained from the SeizeIT2 dataset (OpenNeuro), which includes multimodal data collected using the wearable Sensor Dot device. EEG, ECG, and EMG signals were acquired at a sampling rate of 250 Hz, while accelerometer and gyroscope (ACC/GYR) signals were sampled at 25 Hz [17].

A total of 50 patients were selected via simple random sampling (approximately 40% of the dataset), ensuring a 90% confidence level. All annotated ictal events were extracted and paired with non-ictal (background) segments from the same patient, maintaining class balance across the sample.

2.2 Signal Preprocessing

To preserve physiologically relevant components, modality-specific preprocessing steps were applied. A 50 Hz notch filter and a fourth-order Butterworth band-pass filter were used with the following configurations: EEG signals were filtered between 1–40 Hz to retain brain activity characteristics [18]; ECG signals between 0.5–40 Hz, to preserve P-QRS-T waves; and EMG signals between 20–100 Hz, to capture muscle activation. For ACC/GYR signals, a 0.1–10 Hz range was selected in order to match movement dynamics without overlapping with powerline noise. All signals were segmented into synchronized time windows for further analysis.

2.3 Descriptive, Inferential and Multimodal Correlation Analysis

An integrated statistical analysis was performed per event and modality, where three basic metrics were computed: mean, standard deviation, and amplitude range [19]. Once grouped by signal type and class, these metrics were visualized through time-series plots and boxplots.

To compare distributions between ictal and non-ictal states, the non-parametric Mann–Whitney U test was applied, as data did not follow a normal distribution [12]. The null hypothesis (H_0) assumed no difference between distributions, while the alternative hypothesis (H_1) suggested a significant divergence. Effect sizes were calculated using Cliff's Delta to quantify the magnitude of observed differences [13].

Furthermore, Pearson correlation matrices were computed per patient and event to explore multimodal interactions. Signal pairs with absolute correlation coefficients $|r| \geq 0{,}15$ were retained to identify physiologically meaningful associations linked to seizure occurrence [14].

2.4 Development of a Simple Automatic Classification Model

As a proof of concept, a binary classification model was developed using only the extracted statistical features. The dataset was balanced using SMOTE, and a Random Forest classifier was implemented without hyperparameter tuning due to its ability to handle nonlinear relationships and its robustness to noise [15, 16].

The model was evaluated by modality using standard performance metrics such as accuracy, precision, recall and F1-score. While the model is exploratory in nature, it aims to demonstrate the discriminative power of simple statistical features in seizure detection.

3   Results

The results confirm that simple statistical metrics can consistently differentiate between ictal and non-ictal states across multimodal physiological signals. Findings are organized into four subsections: descriptive analysis of physiological metrics, inferential analysis using non-parametric tests, multimodal correlation analysis, and an automatic classification model.

3.1   Descriptive Analysis

A representative ictal event from a randomly selected patient was analyzed to visualize signal differences relative to non-ictal periods. As shown in Fig. 2, EEG and EMG signals exhibited greater intensity and oscillatory activity during the seizure episode.

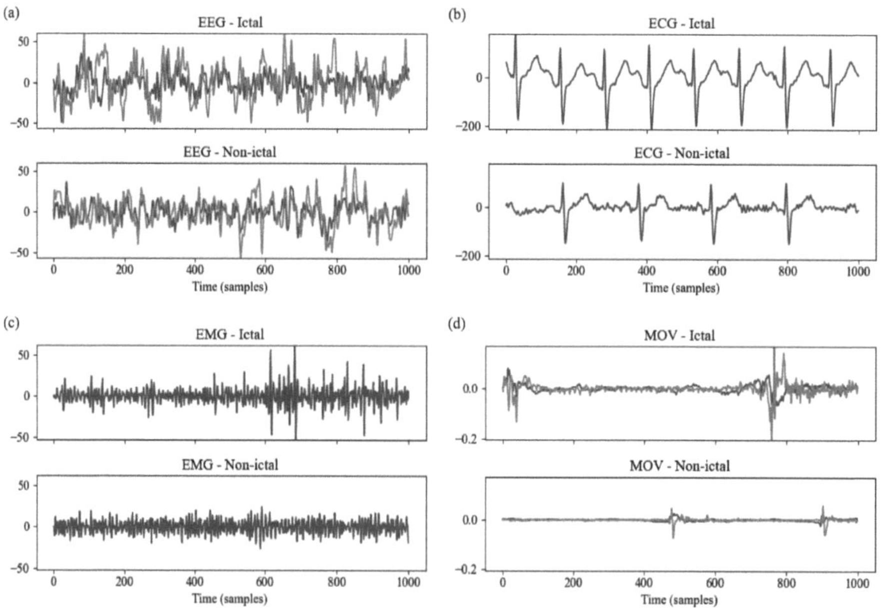

Fig. 2. Visual comparison between ictal and non-ictal events across modalities for a representative patient. (a) EEG signals from two sensors: BTEleft SD (orange) and CROSStop SD (blue). (b) ECG signals. (c) EMG signals. (d) Accelerometer and gyroscope signals (ACC Z and GYR A). Y-axis values are expressed in microvolts (µV). (Color figure online)

From the preprocessed dataset, three statistical metrics (mean, standard deviation, and amplitude range) were calculated for each signal. As summarized in Table 1, the standard deviation tended to increase during ictal states across all modalities. Notably, the amplitude range was generally higher in non-ictal periods, except in movement signals.

Table 1. Summary statistics of metrics by modality and class

Modality	Class	Mean (µV)	Standard deviation (µV)	Amplitude range (µV)
ECG	Ictal	−0,09 ± 2,65	120,15 ± 160,8	1420,59 ± 1646,16
	Non-Ictal	−0,0 ± 0,01	82,3 ± 60,81	4997,53 ± 4009,21
EEG	Ictal	−0,01 ± 0,36	59,88 ± 111,76	970,32 ± 2125,71
	Non-Ictal	−0,0 ± 0,01	39,2 ± 38,22	4716,88 ± 4304,05
EMG	Ictal	0,0 ± 0,05	115,27 ± 143,71	2259,11 ± 2547,89
	Non-Ictal	−0,0 ± 0,0	66,24 ± 100,37	6932,91 ± 3803,45
MOV	Ictal	0,0 ± 0,06	0,07 ± 0,75	0,66 ± 5,82
	Non-Ictal	−0,0 ± 0,0	0,05 ± 0,35	2,03 ± 11,12

The distribution of amplitude range across signal modalities revealed clear interclass differences in EEG, ECG and EMG signals (Fig. 3). In contrast, movement signals exhibited low variability and limited visual separation between classes.

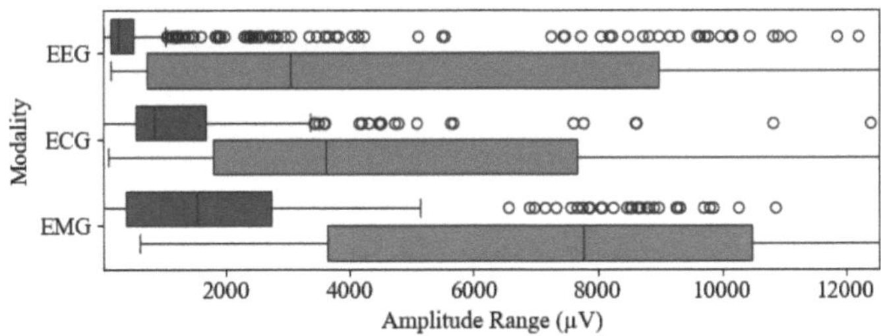

Fig. 3. Boxplot of amplitude range for EEG, ECG, and EMG signals during ictal (blue) and non-ictal (orange) states. (Color figure online)

3.2 Inferential Analysis

The Mann–Whitney U test revealed statistically significant differences in amplitude range and standard deviation across all modalities. No significant differences were found for the mean.

Effect size estimation using Cliff's Delta indicated a strong effect for amplitude range, highlighting consistent distributional shifts during ictal events (Fig. 4). This metric proved particularly sensitive for EEG and EMG signals.

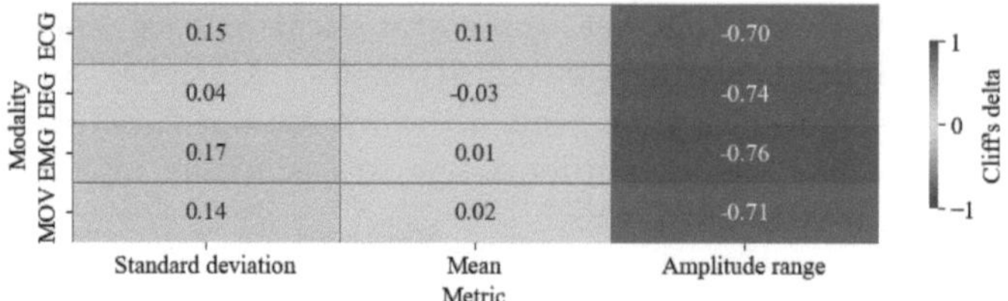

Fig. 4. Effect size (Cliff's Delta) for class differences by modality and metric. Values close to 1 indicate strong effect; values near 0 indicate no effect.

3.3 Multimodal Correlation Between Physiological Signals

During seizure episodes, positive correlations emerged between movement-related and EEG signals (Fig. 5). These relations were weak or absent in non-ictal segments, suggesting a distinctive pattern of physiological coupling associated with seizure activity.

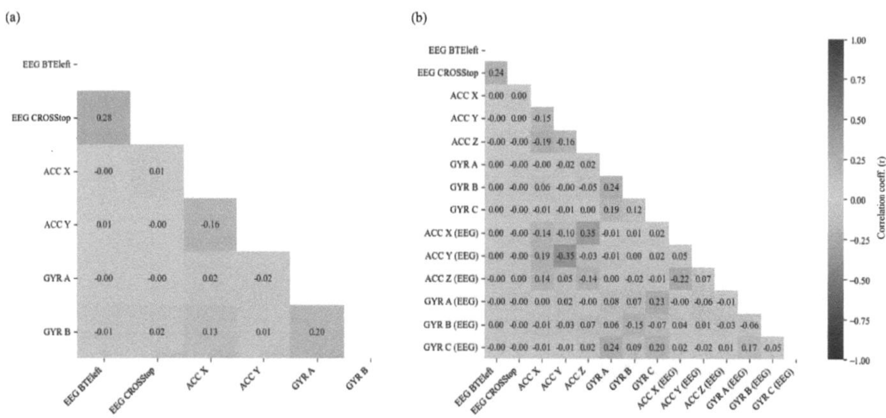

Fig. 5. Pearson correlation matrices between selected channels for (a) ictal and (b) non-ictal events. Channels were included if they exhibited absolute correlation $|r| \geq 0{,}15$ with at least one other signal during any event. Signals include EEG channels (BTEleft, CROSStop), accelerometer (ACC X, Y, Z), gyroscope (GYR A, B, C), and derived EEG movement features. Stronger correlations were observed during ictal events, particularly between EEG and movement signals.

3.4 Random Forest Model

The Random Forest model demonstrated reliable classification performance using only basic statistical features. As presented in Table 2, EEG, ECG, and EMG modalities yielded F1-scores above 0,75; with EEG achieving the highest value (F1 = 0,79). EMG performance was slightly lower (F1 = 0,75), reflecting a just higher variability across events.

Combining EEG, ECG, and EMG features into a multimodal input wielded a competitive F1-score of 0.76, showing that even with simple features, multimodal fusion remains effective for seizure detection.

Table 2. Performance of the Random Forest model by modality using basic statistical features.

Modality	Accuracy	Precision	Recall	F1-score
EEG	0,79	0,78	0,81	0,79
ECG	0,76	0,75	0,79	0,77
EMG	0,75	0,74	0,77	0,75
MOV	0,75	0,74	0,79	0,76
EEG + ECG + EMG	0,76	0,75	0,77	0,76

4   Discussion

This study assessed the discriminative potential of simple statistical metrics derived from EEG, ECG, EMG, and movement signals. An increase in both standard deviation and amplitude range was observed during seizures in brain and muscle signals, reflecting heightened neurophysiological activation [20]. Among all features, amplitude range came up as the most sensitive metric, exhibiting statistically significant differences across all modalities. In contrast, the mean failed to distinguish between ictal and non-ictal states, aligning with previous studies that have highlighted the limitations of first-order statistics in non-stationary biomedical signals [21].

Cliff's Delta further confirmed the relevance of amplitude range, with strong effects observed in EMG ($\Delta \approx 0.76$) and EEG ($\Delta \approx 0.74$) signals, indicating robust distributional differences. As emphasized in the literature, this type of metric is essential to evaluate the clinical usefulness of features in automated systems [22].

The multimodal correlation analysis revealed increased coupling during ictal states, especially between EEG and movement signals. This suggests a functional reorganization of the nervous system during seizures, contrasting with the greater physiological variability observed in non-ictal periods [23]. These findings support the idea that integrating multimodal signals could enhance the sensitivity of detection systems by exploiting the complementarity between modalities.

The exploratory Random Forest model demonstrated acceptable performance using EEG, ECG, and EMG signals. However, the movement signals showed lower precision, potentially due to artifacts and baseline variability [24]. In addition, the multimodal model showed adequate performance (F1 = 0.76) in comparison to the individual ones, which exhibit that multimodal combination can be useful when a device fails individually. These results highlight the value of low-complexity multimodal approaches in preliminary stages [25]. Future research should incorporate more advanced architectures, feature-level or decision-level fusion strategies [4,26], and explore preictal states, spectral and nonlinear analyses, and validation in larger clinical cohorts.

References

1. Pérez Navarro, V.M., Cánovas Iniesta, M., Palazón Cabanes, B., Navarro Lozano, M.: Epilepsia y desigualdad: descripción demográfica y análisis de la dificultad para el acceso a recursos avanzados en una población de un área de salud pequeña. RevNeurol **77**(11), 259 (2023). https://doi.org/10.33588/rn.7711.2023262
2. Manole, A.M., Sibu, C.A., Mititelu, M.R., Vasiliu, O., Lorusso, L., Sirbu, O.M.: State of the art and challenges in epilepsy - a narrative review. JPM **13**(4), 623 (2023). https://doi.org/10.3390/jpm13040623
3. Devarajan, K., Bagyaraj, S., Balasampath, V., Jyostna, E., Jayasri, K.: EEG-based epilepsy detection and prediction. IJET **6**(3), 212–216 (2014). https://doi.org/10.7763/IJET.2014.V6.698
4. Zurdo-Tabernero, M., Canal-Alonso, Á., De La Prieta, F., Rodríguez, S., Prieto, J., Corchado, J.M.: An overview of machine learning and deep learning techniques for predicting epileptic seizures. J. Integr. Bioinform. **20**(4), 20230002 (2024). https://doi.org/10.1515/jib-2023-0002
5. Pillai, J., Sperling, M.R.: Interictal EEG and the diagnosis of epilepsy. Epilepsia **47**(s1), 14–22 (2006). https://doi.org/10.1111/j.1528-1167.2006.00654.x
6. Ramírez-Campos, J., Núñez-Velázquez, M., Cárdenas-Rojo, N., Sevilla-Castillo, R.A., Palacios-Saucedo, G.C.: Confiabilidad intra e interobservador de la lectura del EEG en pacientes pediátricos con alteraciones neurológicas. Rev. Med. Inst. Mex. Seguro Soc. (2014)
7. Zhang, X., Zhang, X., Huang, Q., Chen, F.: A review of epilepsy detection and prediction methods based on EEG signal processing and deep learning. Front. Neurosci. **18**, 1468967 (2024). https://doi.org/10.3389/fnins.2024.1468967
8. Yassin, A., et al.: Diagnostic value of electrocardiogram during routine electroencephalogram. Seizure **89**, 19–23 (2021). https://doi.org/10.1016/j.seizure.2021.04.016
9. Borujeny, G., Yazdi, M., Keshavarz-Haddad, A., Borujeny, A.: Detection of epileptic seizure using wireless sensor networks. J. Med. Signals Sens. **3**(2), 63 (2013). https://doi.org/10.4103/2228-7477.114373
10. Zhao, S., et al.: A Systematic Review of Machine Learning Methods for Multimodal EEG Data in Clinical Application. arXiv (2024). https://doi.org/10.48550/arXiv.2501.08585
11. Traversaro, F., Redelico, F.: Confidence intervals and hypothesis testing for the permutation entropy with an application to epilepsy. Commun. Nonlinear Sci. Numer. Simul. **57**, 388–401 (2018). https://doi.org/10.1016/j.cnsns.2017.10.013
12. Woldman, W., et al.: Dynamic network properties of the interictal brain determine whether seizures appear focal or generalised. Sci. Rep. **10**(1), 7043 (2020). https://doi.org/10.1038/s41598-020-63430-9
13. Cliff, N.: Dominance statistics: ordinal analyses to answer ordinal questions. Psychol. Bull. **114**(3), 494–509 (1993). https://doi.org/10.1037/0033-2909.114.3.494

14. Quintero-Rincon, A., D'Giano, C., Risk, M.: Epileptic seizure prediction using Pearson's product-moment correlation coefficient of a linear classifier from generalized Gaussian modeling. Neurol. Argent. **10**(4), 210–217 (2018). https://doi.org/10.1016/j.neuarg.2018.06.004
15. Tzimourta, K.D., Tzallas, A.T., Giannakeas, N., Astrakas, L.G., Tsalikakis, D.G., Angelidis, P., Tsipouras, M.G.: A robust methodology for classification of epileptic seizures in EEG signals. Heal. Technol. **9**(2), 135–142 (2018). https://doi.org/10.1007/s12553-018-0265-z
16. Wang, X., Gong, G., Li, N., Qiu, S.: Detection analysis of epileptic EEG using a novel random forest model combined with grid search optimization. Front. Hum. Neurosci. **13**, 52 (2019). https://doi.org/10.3389/fnhum.2019.00052
17. Bhagubai, M., et al.: SeizeIT2: Wearable Dataset of Patients with Focal Epilepsy. arXiv (2025). https://doi.org/10.48550/arXiv.2502.01224
18. Bomatter, P., Paillard, J., Garces, P., Hipp, J., Engemann, D.-A.: Machine learning of brain-specific biomarkers from EEG. EBioMedicine **106**, 105259 (2024). https://doi.org/10.1016/j.ebiom.2024.105259
19. Aslam, M.H., et al.: Classification of EEG signals for prediction of epileptic seizures. Appl. Sci. **12**(14), 7251 (2022). https://doi.org/10.3390/app12147251
20. Conradsen, I., Wolf, P., Sams, T., Sorensen, H.B.D., Beniczky, S.: Patterns of muscle activation during generalized tonic and tonic-clonic epileptic seizures. Epilepsia **52**(11), 2125–2132 (2011). https://doi.org/10.1111/j.1528-1167.2011.03286.x
21. Seijas, C., Villazana, S., Montilla, G., Pérez, E., Montilla, R.: Detector de Neuropatologías en EEG usando Estadísticas de Orden Superior y Aprendizaje Profundo. RevIngUC **28**(1), 141–151 (2021). https://doi.org/10.54139/revinguc.v28i1.14
22. Macbeth, G., Razumiejczyk, E., Ledesma, R.D.: Cliff's delta calculator: a nonparametric effect size program for two groups of observations. Univ. Psychol. **10(2), Art. 2**, 10.11144/Javeriana.upsy10–2.cdcp (2011)
23. Glaba, P., et al.: EEG phase synchronization during absence seizures. Front. Neuroinform. **17**, 1169584 (2023). https://doi.org/10.3389/fninf.2023.1169584
24. Böttcher, S., et al.: Effects of epileptic seizures on the quality of biosignals recorded from wearables. Epilepsia **65**(12), 3513–3525 (2024). https://doi.org/10.1111/epi.18138
25. Zhang, Y., Zhou, W., Yuan, Q., Wu, Q.: A low computation cost method for seizure prediction. Epilepsy Res. **108**(8), 1357–1366 (2014). https://doi.org/10.1016/j.eplepsyres.2014.06.007
26. Kim, H., Lee, S.M., Choi, S.: Automatic sleep stages classification using multi-level fusion. Biomed. Eng. Lett. **12**(4), 413–420 (2022). https://doi.org/10.1007/s13534-022-00244-w

Detection of Epileptogenic Patterns in Thalamic Neurostimulated Signals Through Spatial Deep Attention

Martín Robins[1,2]($\boxtimes$) , Valentina Gigy[1,2], R. Mark Richardson[3] ,
and Victoria Peterson[1]

[1] Instituto de Matemática Aplicada del Litoral, IMAL, UNL-CONICET, Santa Fe, Argentina
mrobins@santafe-conicet.gov.ar
[2] Escuela de Ingeniería Biomédica, Facultad de Ciencias Exactas, Físicas y Naturales,
Universidad Nacional de Córdoba, Córdoba, Argentina
[3] Department of Neurosurgery, Massachusetts General Hospital, Harvard Medical School,
Boston, MA, USA

Abstract. Patients with drug-resistant epilepsy can be treated with the Responsive Neurostimulation (RNS) system. This system has the ability to sense the electrical activity of the brain and provide stimulation when epileptiform patterns are detected. Patients implanted with the RNS system in the thalamus experience longer periods of stimulation. Since the implanted electrodes have a dual function of sensing and stimulating, patients with RNS in the thalamus show recordings with significant data information loss. Consequently, deep learning algorithms developed to analyze the presence of epileptogenic patterns in RNS recordings have shown decreased performance when evaluated in thalamic patients. This study aims to enhance the detection capability of epileptogenic patterns in a deep neural network (iESPnet) for thalamic patients by integrating a spatial attention mechanism called Dynamic Spatial Filtering (DSF) into the learning process. Various experiments were conducted to determine if the combined use of DSF and iESPnet has the potential to improve the detection capacity of epileptogenic patterns. A database of 30 patients implanted with RNS was utilized. The results demonstrate that the integration of the attention mechanism has the potential to enhance the network's detection capabilities, achieving relative improvements of up to 30% compared to the original network architecture. Thus, this work defines an explorative path to improve personalized treatment for patients with refractory epilepsy through the automation of epileptogenic pattern detection, significantly reducing the workload of specialists.

Keywords: Drug-resistant epilepsy · iEEG · Neurostimulation · Deep Learning · Dynamic Spatial Filtering · Thalamic Implants

1 Introduction

Epilepsy is a chronic neurological disorder characterized by recurrent, unprovoked seizures [1]. A significant subset of patients continues to experience seizures despite receiving appropriate pharmacological treatment, a condition known as drug-resistant

A. Talevi and V. Rosa Cota (Eds.): LAWCN 2025, CCIS 2734, pp. 12–22, 2026.
https://doi.org/10.1007/978-3-032-14664-9_2

epilepsy. The Responsive Neurostimulation System (RNS) is the first and only bidirectional device specifically designed to monitor and treat patients with drug-resistant epilepsy [2]. It continuously records brain activity using intracranial electroencephalography (iEEG) and delivers stimulation to one or two seizure onset zones in response to detected epileptiform activity. The programmable parameters of the RNS detection and stimulation algorithms are adjusted based on each patient's clinical evaluation and ongoing therapeutic response [2, 3].

However, this personalized approach requires clinicians to review large volumes of data in order to identify intracranial electrographic seizure patterns (iESP). This challenge underscores the need for tools that can facilitate data analysis, particularly given the complexity of interpretation and the time-consuming nature of manual review [4]. In response to this demand, the application of deep learning algorithms for the automatic detection of iESP represents a promising strategy for processing large-scale datasets that could enhance patient monitoring. In addition, such tools may help reduce the workload of clinical experts, particularly in time-constrained settings, by allowing them to focus more effectively on the management of personalized therapies.

In this context, Peterson et al. developed iESPnet, a deep neural network designed to detect epileptiform patterns in intracranial EEG. iESPnet combines convolutional and recurrent neural networks and operates on time–frequency representations of iEEG signals recorded from the RNS system. The model achieves a mean detection accuracy of 90% and an onset time prediction error of approximately 3.4 s [4], iESP detection values comparable to those found between experts.

Due to the nature of the RNS system, data loss occurs during stimulation intervals. Such data loss particularly compromises signal quality in a specific group of patients with thalamic RNS implantation, where due to their longer stimulation time, the automatic identification of iESP is hard to accomplish.

In fact, the loss of information in patients with thalamic implants reduces the network's accuracy, highlighting the need to improve the detection system to effectively handle the complexity of these signals. Enhancing the system's performance under these conditions is essential to support the personalization of therapy for this patient population.

In the domain of surface EEG, it is common to encounter missing signal segments or even the complete loss of individual channels. To address this issue, a machine learning architecture has recently been proposed to dynamically transform artifactual signals in real time before being passed to a subsequent model. This architecture performs adaptive adjustments through the use of dynamic spatial filtering (DSF) techniques, a form of spatial attention, which allows adaptability to signal fluctuations and artifacts [5].

Aiming to develop automatic tools to identify iESP regardless of electrode placement within the RNS system, here we propose to combine Dynamic Spatial Filtering (DSF) with iESPnet to improve the detection of epileptogenic patterns, particularly in patients implanted with thalamic electrodes. This study is a step forward in the design of computed-based systems that support iESP identification from thalamic RNS iEEG recordings.

2   Materials and Methods

2.1   Patients and Data

iEEG signals from 30 patients implanted with the RNS System (NeuroPace) at the University of Pittsburgh Medical Center (Pittsburgh, PA, USA) were used in this study. The recordings were obtained between 2015 and 2020 under an institutional review board-approved protocol. The iEEG data were reviewed by an experienced epilepsy surgery neurophysiologist, who was responsible for identifying the presence of epileptogenic patterns and marking the seizure onset in the corresponding cases [6]. The dataset includes a total of 42,498 recording segments, each containing four channels monitoring brain electrical activity from different regions. Of the total recordings, 9,476 contain the label provided by the specialist indicating the presence of at least one epileptogenic pattern in that recording. Among the selected patients, 17 were female and 13 male. Electrode implantation sites were distributed according to etiology as follows: cortex (10), hippocampus (7), thalamus (5), cortical malformation (4), and mixed combinations such as hippocampus–cortex (3) and thalamus–cortex (1). Each segment consists of a time-varying voltage signal reflecting brain activity in a period of at least 60 s. These signals were bandpass filtered between 4 and 125 Hz and sampled at 250 Hz.

2.2   Data Preprocessing

To train the model, 90-s segments of iEEG recordings were used. Recordings longer than 90 s were divided into non-overlapping segments of this length, while shorter recordings were zero-padded to match the typical 90-s segment duration. Each training segment consisted of 22,500 samples (90 s x 250) per channel and was associated with a label indicating the presence or absence of seizure-related activity, as well as the time of seizure onset, when available.

2.3   Electrographic Seizure Detection Network

iESPnet (intracranial Electrographic Seizure Pattern Network) is a deep neural network specifically designed for the detection of epileptogenic patterns in iEEG signals from patients implanted with the RNS system [6]. The network uses time-frequency representation of the iEEG signals, piled along the channel axis to conform a 3D representation of the data (channel, time, frequency). In order to accomplish both the iESP identification and onset estimation, the net is trained to quantify at each sample time the probability of an iESP onset to occur. For this, a continuous label is used, where seizure onsets are masked with smooth Gaussian bells around the time onset.

The network architecture combines six convolutional layers (CNNs), three bidirectional recurrent layers (GRUs), and two fully connected layers. The CNNs are organized into blocks: the first three layers extract temporal, frequency, and time-frequency features, followed by three additional layers arranged in ResCNN (residual CNN) blocks to extract deeper features. The GRUs, with decreasing latent dimensions (150, 100, and 50), process sequential information over the 90-s iEEG segments, leveraging the memory capabilities of recurrent networks to enable the model to learn the temporal evolution of an iESP. Finally, the fully connected layers, together with a SoftMax activation function, allow for the estimation of the probability of an iESP onset at each sample point in the signal. The network includes a total of 1,654,837 parameters [4].

2.4 The Spatial Attention Mechanism

The Dynamic Spatial Filtering (DSF) method aims to address the challenge of working with EEG signals that exhibit information loss. DSF can be regarded as an advanced solution that not only filters noise but also dynamically adapts its spatial filters in real time to optimize the quality of the captured signal, thereby enabling a more accurate representation of relevant brain activity [5].

As illustrated in Fig. 1, the DSF relies on the spatial covariance matrices of each input signal so as to capture the spatial relationships between the different channels. Such covariance matrices are then vectorized and processed by a two-layer Multi-Layer Perceptron (MLP). The weights of the MLP are in fact the spatial filters that would dynamically adapt to signal temporal variations. As typically done in signal processing, the learned spatial filters can be applied to the original signal and thus, obtain a filtered version that maximizes the signal-to-noise ratio. The filtered signal can then be used as input to another model, such as a neural network designed for a specific downstream task [5]. As shown in Fig. 1, the dynamic spatial filtering can mathematically be described by the following equation:

$$DSF(X) = W_{DSF}X + b_{DSF} \tag{1}$$

where X is a data matrix with C channels and T sample points, W_{DSF} is a matrix of size $C \times C$ whose columns vectors represent the spatial filters, and b_{DSF} is the bias term. The final aim of DSF is to assign different weights to each channel based on its contribution to the classification task, allowing it to ignore or attenuate corrupted channels while preserving relevant spatial information [5].

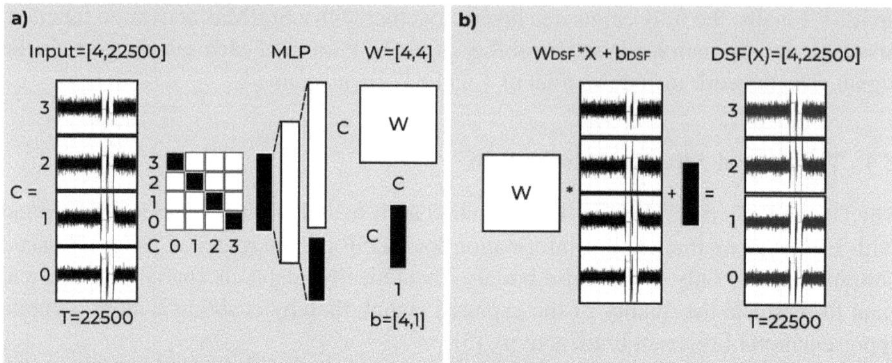

Fig. 1. The Dynamic Spatial Filtering process for iEEG-RNS data. a) From raw data to spatial filters. Given a raw iEEG, the diagonal of its covariance matrix is used as input to a two-layer multilayer perceptron (MLP). This network learns a spatial filter matrix W and a bias vector b that will later be used to transform the signal. Here, MLP stands for multilayer perceptron, C indicates the number of channels, and T represents the number of time samples. b) Online dynamic spatial filtering. The learned matrix W and bias vector b are applied to the original signal to obtain a filtered version that maximizes the signal-to-noise ratio. Here, DSF stands for Dynamic Spatial Filtering.

2.5   Robust Automatic iESP Identification with Dynamic Spatial Filtering

Thalamic iEEG recordings acquired by the RNS present longer stimulation artifacts, leading to poor iESPnet detection performance when tested in this patient group. Signal processing steps to gap missing data could be applied to improve signal quality. Leveraging learnable and automatic algorithms, here we propose an innovative solution for the detection of iESPs by combining DSF with iESPnet in a joint optimization procedure. The final number of trainable parameters is 1,654,957.

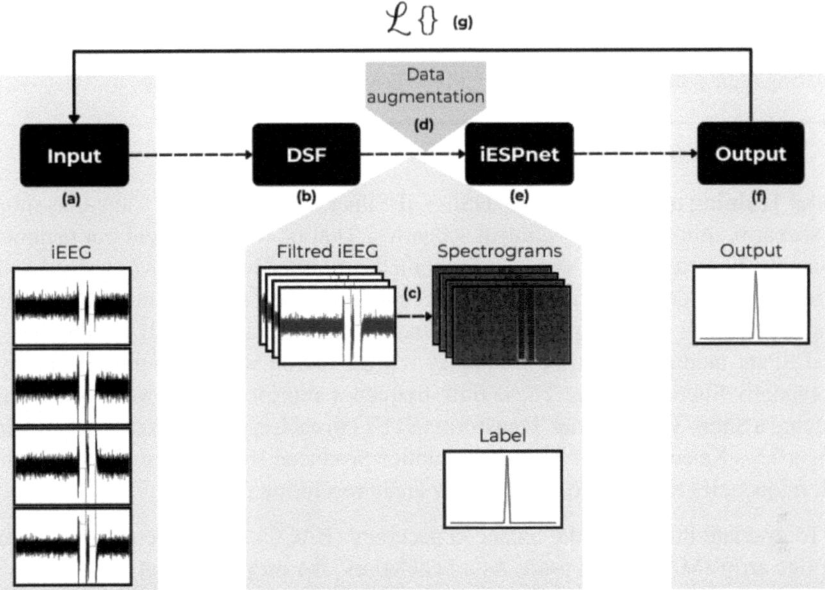

Fig. 2. Diagram of the proposed approach. The process begins with iEEG signals (a) as input, which are first processed by the Dynamic Spatial Filtering (DSF) module (b). The filtered signals are then converted into spectrograms (c), and data augmentation techniques are applied (d) to improve model robustness. These representations are used to train iESPnet (e), a neural network designed for deep feature extraction. The network outputs a continuous prediction (f) for the detection of epileptogenic patterns, guided by a single loss function (g) that optimizes the entire pipeline.

As shown in Fig. 2a, the workflow begins with the 4 channel 90s length raw iEEG data segment. Next, the DSF module performs the denoising process through spatial attention, analyzing inter-channel relationships to determine which information should be emphasized and which should be attenuated. This analysis enables the creation of a dynamic filter that adjusts in real time its weights according to the characteristics of the incoming signal. The resulting filter is then applied to the input signal, producing a transformed output with same dimensionality, but spatially enhanced (Fig. 2b).

After the filtering stage, the iEEG signals undergo global normalization. Subsequently, the signals are transformed into spectrograms in order to be processed by iESPnet (Fig. 2c).

In favor of fostering generalization capabilities, and following their original implementation, data augmentation strategies are used before training the iESPnet module (Fig. 2d). In particular TimeMasking, FrequencyMasking and Channel Permutation are used to duplicate the training data size. To keep the double functionality of iESPnet in identification and onset iESP prediction, the model is trained with the continuous level, as depicted in Fig. 2e, leading to a continuous output that predicts the probability of a seizure pattern to start (Fig. 2f).

To perform the joint optimization, the model parameters are adjusted end-to-end with the same loss function, as shown in Fig. 2g. Two optimizers, and two learning rate schedulers that coordinate the parameter update process are used. This ensures that both the DSF module and the iESPnet network are optimized in a coordinated manner, adjusting their parameters to improve the overall system performance.

2.6   Experiments and Results

Model Training and Evaluation. DSF + iESPnet was trained on a leave-one-subject-out scenario, mimicking real clinical scenarios. That is, for every held out patient, the remaining 29 patients' data were used to train the model. The model was trained to minimize the binary cross-entropy (BCE) loss function at each sample time, using AdamW as optimizer with a learning rate of .001 and a weight decay of .0001 for the DSF and the iESPnet module. The time-frequency representation was computed on-the-fly on the spatially filtered signals. These time-frequency representations were generated by applying a Short-Time Fourier Transform (STFT) to each spatially filtered 90-s segment using a 0.5-s Kaiser window. This segmentation produced 180 time samples per channel, with frequencies ranging from 0 to 60 Hz and a resolution of 0.5 Hz.

To evaluate the model the balanced accuracy (BACC), the F1-score and the mean absolute error (MAE) were used. As a benchmark, the proposed joint architecture was compared to the original iESPnet.

Comparative results in terms of balanced accuracy, F1 score, and MAE are presented in Fig. 3. Thalamic patients are highlighted in blue color; as shown, the use of dynamic spatial filtering has the potential to enhance the detection of epileptogenic patterns.

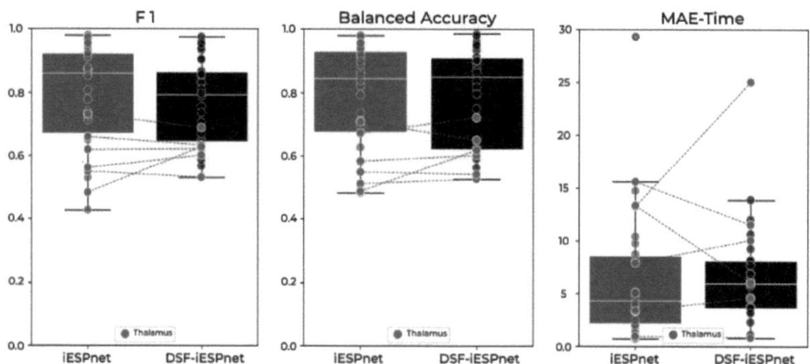

Fig. 3. Impact of dynamic spatial filtering for iESP identification. The proposed architecture (DSF + iESPnet) is compared against the original iESPnet model under a leave-one-subject-out training regime. F1, Balanced accuracy and MAE are used to assess performance. Here every dot represents a patient. Thalamic patients are highlighted in blue.

The Effect of Data Blanks in Model Performance. DSF is a spatial attention module expected to perform real-time denoising dynamically, depending on the degree of information loss in the input data. Given the comparative results between the proposed model and the original network, it is important to analyze whether performance losses or improvements can be explained based on certain data characteristics specific to each patient.

Given that DSF can be thought of as a pre-processing step aiming to address data loss, two key aspects that involve missing data were quantified. On the one hand, the stimulation times defined during a programming epoch were considered. Since the RNS parameters are adjusted during each medical visit to ensure better monitoring and treatment of the patient, the aim was to determine whether there is a relationship between the stimulation time parameter and the DSF's ability to enhance ESP detection. In each programming epoch, the stimulation time can be adjusted, generating variability in the amount of data blanks in the iEEG recordings. Thus, for each iEEG segment, the average stimulation time was calculated, defined as the average length of periods with data loss.

On the other hand, due to the way the nets are trained, input data may contain zero padded segments when the recording duration is shorter than 90 s. That is, we want to study whether the zero padding step affects model performance. For each iEEG recording, the length of the padding required to reach 90 s was calculated. This parameter will be referred to as "Z-Padding Time", and can be viewed as a type of data blank for the model.

To determine whether there is any relationship between the proposed model's detection performance and the level of blanks in the input data, correlation analyses were performed across the different metrics. Additionally, the relative performance change of the proposed model (DSF + iESPnet) compared to the original one (iESPnet) was computed in order to assess whether positive or negative changes can be explained by these descriptive variables of the input data. That is, the relative balance accuracy and F1 score computed as the expected gain between applying DSF from the original formulation was computed.

Figure 4 displays a paired-variable scatterplot, illustrating whether or not there is a relationship between model performance and input data quality. This figure shows the average stimulation and z-padding times across all recordings of a given patient. A color code is used to easily distinguish thalamic patients from the rest. As expected, patients with thalamic implants exhibit longer stimulation times, and consequently, model performance tends to be among the lowest, reinforcing the hypothesis that stimulation time indeed impacts performance. Nevertheless, when analyzing the relative change in balanced accuracy, it is interesting to see that for the thalamic patients the proposed model consistently yields similar or superior performance compared to the original model. This analysis shows that, despite the increased contamination of the data by stimulation artifacts, the greater the benefit obtained from using the spatial attention mechanism.

Regarding the amount of zero-padded time, it is notable how iESP detection, measured via F1-Score, tends to decrease as the number of zero-padded time samples increases. When analyzing data from thalamic patients, it becomes evident that they belong to the group of patients with a moderate to large amount of zero-padded data.

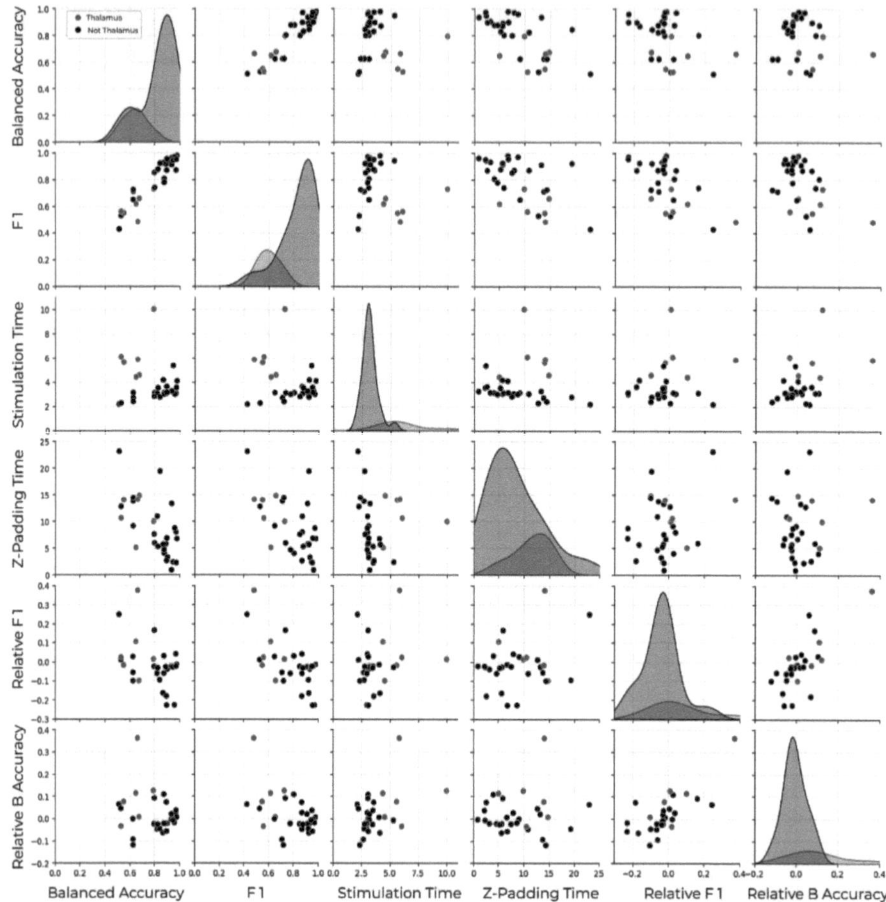

Fig. 4. Graphical summary of the relationship between variables. Each point represents a patient. Stimulation and padding times are the average value across all recordings of a given patient. Patients from the target group (thalamic) are distinguished from the rest.

3   Discussion

The present study aimed to address the challenge of detecting epileptogenic patterns in thalamic signals by combining signal processing techniques with deep learning models in a jointly optimized procedure. Specifically, the Dynamic Spatial Filtering was implemented and evaluated in combination with the iESPnet architecture to improve the system's robustness to data loss, which is frequently observed in patients with thalamic implants of the Responsive Neurostimulation System.

The results suggest that the proposed architecture maintains the baseline model's overall accuracy trend without significantly compromising predictive performance. This is a critical consideration for the technique's potential clinical applications. However, although the results are not significantly different, the slight decrease in F1 score might reflect a reduced ability of the model to accurately detect positive events, particularly the presence of epileptogenic patterns. This drop may be due to the model tending to improve non-event detection at the expense of sensitivity to positive events. This appears to be related to the model prioritizing non-event detection and possibly using silent or inactive segments as references for its predictions, which affects its sensitivity to critical events.

While the overall accuracy remained stable, the proposed model tends to improve balanced accuracy for the thalamic patients. An overall accuracy around. 85 has the potential to alleviate specialists' workload by reducing the amount of data requiring manual review. The model's ability to reliably identify irrelevant records allows experts to focus on the most critical segments, enhancing diagnostic efficiency.

The analysis of the relationship between performance variables and data quality quantifiers allowed understanding the proposed model's capacity. It was evidenced that higher stimulation time correlates with performance metric deterioration. Although expected, this result suggests significant levels of data corruption that cannot be fully corrected by the DSF algorithm. This represents an important limitation of the method. However, when comparing these results to those obtained with the original technique, a notable improvement in classification accuracy is observed. Although the limited number of patients prevents robust statistical analysis, these results indicate a positive trend. This improvement is especially significant in cases with more complex data conditions, suggesting the proposed strategy can more effectively handle challenging situations.

To date, only a few other studies apply deep learning techniques for detecting epileptogenic patterns in iEEG signals acquired by the RNS system. In fact, the use of this system for treating thalamic patients is new and emerging [7, 8]. Existing deep learning methods in the literature for iESP detection in iEEG acquired via RNS do not include patients with RNS implanted in the thalamus [4, 9, 10]. Nevertheless, missing data handling for detection problems is an area of study in scalp EEG signals. Thus, while this work addressed the solution with widely used spatial filtering techniques for scalp EEG, other methods could be explored, such as inpainting or alternative signal filtering mechanisms [11, 12]. Similarly, DSF can be considered a spatial attention mechanism within the neural network. Other deep learning-derived techniques could be explored, such as generative or adversarial models, to name a few. However, choosing DSF over other possible solutions enables building a model of similar complexity to the existing one with the potential to perform denoising alongside the final detection task, which is convenient for model design, optimization, and subsequent use.

4   Conclusion

This work presents the integration of Dynamic Spatial Filtering (DSF) with the iESPnet neural network to detect epileptogenic patterns in thalamic iEEG recordings registered with the RNS device. Although this combination does not fully resolve the challenges posed by this type of signal, it shows comparative or superior performance to the original model, particularly in datasets affected by stimulation-related data blanks. Moreover, by improving the automatic identification of electrographic seizure patterns, the proposed approach contributes to reducing the manual workload of clinical specialists, facilitating more efficient and focused decision-making in personalized therapy. Future work should aim to optimize the model's balance between precision and sensitivity, enhance the dynamic adaptability of the DSF module under varying levels of data loss, and explore more informed validation strategies based on clinical characteristics. In addition, leveraging the full covariance matrix, including inter-channel correlations, may provide further improvements in performance, particularly in highly synchronized brain activity contexts.

Acknowledgments. This work used computational resources provided by UNC Supercómputo (CCAD) – Universidad Nacional de Córdoba (https://supercomputo.unc.edu.ar), which are part of SNCAD, República Argentina.

Disclosure of Interests. R. M. Richardson has served as a consultant for NeuroPace. The rest of the co-authors have no competing interests to declare.

References

1. Epilepsia - OPS/OMS | Organización Panamericana de la Salud. https://www.paho.org/es/temas/epilepsia. Accessed 22 Jun 2025
2. Skarpaas, T.L., Jarosiewicz, B., Morrell, M.J.: Brain-responsive neurostimulation for epilepsy (RNS ® System). Epilepsy Res. **153**, 68–70 (2019)
3. Rønborg, S.N., et al.: Acute effects of brain-responsive neurostimulation in drug-resistant partial onset epilepsy. Clin. Neurophysiol. **132**, 1209–1220 (2021). https://doi.org/10.1016/j.clinph.2021.03.013
4. Peterson, V., et al.: Deep net detection and onset prediction of electrographic seizure patterns in responsive neurostimulation. Epilepsia **64**, 2056–2069 (2023). https://doi.org/10.1111/EPI.17666
5. Banville, H., et al.: Robust learning from corrupted EEG with dynamic spatial filtering. Neuroimage **251** (2022). https://doi.org/10.1016/J.NEUROIMAGE.2022.118994
6. Sisterson, N.D., et al.: Closed-loop brain stimulation for drug-resistant epilepsy: towards an evidence-based approach to personalized medicine. Neurotherapeutics **16**, 119–127 (2019)
7. Venkatesh, P., Wolfe, C., Lega, B.: Neuromodulation of the anterior thalamus: current approaches and opportunities for the future. Curr. Res. Neurobiol. **5** (2023)
8. Sisterson, N.D., et al.: Responsive neurostimulation of the thalamus improves seizure control in idiopathic generalised epilepsy: initial case series. J. Neurol. Neurosurg. Psychiatry **93**, 491–498 (2022). https://doi.org/10.1136/jnnp-2021-327512
9. Arcot Desai, S., et al.: Expert and deep learning model identification of iEEG seizures and seizure onset times. Front. Neurosci. **17** (2023). https://doi.org/10.3389/fnins.2023.1156838
10. Barry, W., Arcot Desai, S., Tcheng, T.K., Morrell, M.J.: A high accuracy electrographic seizure classifier trained using semi-supervised labeling applied to a large spectrogram dataset. Front. Neurosci. **15** (2021). https://doi.org/10.3389/fnins.2021.667373
11. de Cheveigné, A., Arzounian, D.: Robust detrending, rereferencing, outlier detection, and inpainting for multichannel data. Neuroimage **172**, 903–912 (2018). https://doi.org/10.1016/j.neuroimage.2018.01.035
12. Chang, C.Y., Hsu, S.H., Pion-Tonachini, L., Jung, T.P.: Evaluation of Artifact subspace reconstruction for automatic Artifact components removal in multi-channel EEG recordings. IEEE Trans. Biomed. Eng. **67**, 1114–1121 (2020). https://doi.org/10.1109/TBME.2019.2930186

In Silico Screening to Identify Metabotropic Glutamate Receptor 1 Allosteric Modulators Using Ensemble Learning

Maximiliano J. Fallico[1] , Martina Wecera[1] , Cristian Rojas[2] , Alan Talevi[1(✉)] , and Lucas N. Alberca[1]

[1] Laboratorio de Investigación y Desarrollo de Bioactivos (LIDeB), Facultad de Ciencias Exactas, Universidad Nacional de La Plata, La Plata, Argentina
`alantalevi@gmail.com, lucasalberca@gmail.com`
[2] Grupo de Investigación en Quimiometría y QSAR, Facultad de Ciencia y Tecnología, Universidad del Azuay, Cuenca, Ecuador

Abstract. Metabotropic glutamate receptors (mGLuRs) are attractive targets for the development of therapeutics for a diversity of neurological and neuropsychiatric conditions, such as chronic pain, epilepsy, neurodegenerative disorders, addiction disorders, and anxiety. Previous bioinformatic analyses have shown that they have a considerable similarity with taste receptors such as umami and sweet taste receptors, suggesting that relationships between taste and potential pharmacological activity may be established. Here, we have developed and validated classifiers and meta-classifiers capable of identifying mGluR subtype 1 (mGluR1) positive allosteric modulators. The resulting models have been validated via retrospective virtual screening campaigns, with excellent average and early enrichment metrics (area under the Receiver Operating Characteristic curve ≈ 0.99 and BEDROC, $\alpha = 100, > 0.90$), and later applied in prospective virtual screening experiments.

Keywords: metabotropic glutamate receptors. mGluR · ensemble learning · virtual screening

1 Introduction

Metabotropic glutamate receptors (mGluRs) are family C G-protein-coupled receptors involved in the modulation of synaptic transmission and neuronal excitability in the central nervous system. Both orthosteric and allosteric modulators of mGluRs have been proposed as potential treatments for a wide range of neurological and neuropsychiatric disorders, including anxiety, depression, schizophrenia, neurodegenerative conditions, chronic pain, and addiction disorders [1, 2]. The orthosteric site of mGluRs is located within a large extracellular N-terminal domain, termed the Venus flytrap domain (VFD) [1]. Significant efforts have been made to develop agonists and antagonists that interact at the glutamate-binding site to mimic or block the endogenous actions of this neurotransmitter. The high conservation of orthosteric binding sites across mGluR subtypes

© The Author(s), under exclusive license to Springer Nature Switzerland AG 2026
A. Talevi and V. Rosa Cota (Eds.): LAWCN 2025, CCIS 2734, pp. 23–36, 2026.
https://doi.org/10.1007/978-3-032-14664-9_3

has proven to be a critical barrier to the development of subtype-selective ligands [3]. Therefore, considering that allosteric sites are less conserved across different subtypes of these receptors, recent attention has been focused on the possibility of developing selective positive and negative allosteric modulators (PAMs and NAMs, in that order) that would interact at the level of the transmembrane domains (TMDs) [3, 4].

The role of mGluRs in epilepsy and animal models of epilepsy and seizures has long been recognized and investigated [5, 6]. It is interesting to note that, while mGluR antagonists seem to consistently show protective activity in animal models of convulsive seizures, positive effects on the epileptic phenotype were observed when administering selective PAMs [6]. A potential advantage of allosteric mGluR modulators is that, by definition, these molecules modulate receptor function in an activity-dependent manner, requiring glutamate binding to the receptor to elicit (or at last potentiate) their pharmacological activity. Therefore, we expect these drugs to act when receptors are highly activated by endogenous glutamate, and this could improve the safety profile of the therapeutic intervention compared with orthosteric modulators [3, 7].

A few years ago, Talevi et al. observed that various artificial sweeteners exhibited anticonvulsant activity in animal models of seizure [8–10]. They also established the sequence similarity between metabotropic glutamate receptors (including mGluR1 and mGluR5) and one of the subunits (T1R3) of sweet and umami taste receptors [8]. It is interesting to note that the binding site of cyclamate, one of the sweeteners with anticonvulsant action, has been identified in the transmembrane domain of the T1R3 subunit [11], similarly to what has been described for allosteric modulators of mGluRs [12, 13]. This type of structural evidence could provide a foundation for the long-established empirical relationships between taste and therapeutic use [14].

In this work, supervised machine learning was applied to establish relationships between the molecular structure of small molecules and their ability to act as mGluR1 PAMs. The resulting models were used to screen the following databases: a) DrugBank [15] and The Drug Repurposing Hub (DRH) [16], aimed at drug repurposing (i.e., identifying new medical uses for known drugs); and FoodDB [17], which compiles food ingredients or constituents and could serve as a basis for identifying nutraceuticals. Furthermore, considering the possible relationship between sweet taste and antiseizure activity, the ChemTastesDB database (version 2) [18, 19], which compiles 4,075 molecular tastants classified according to their taste characteristics into basic and non-basic tastes, was also screened.

2   Methods

2.1   Dataset Compilation and Curation

A search for mGlu activity data was performed in the ChEMBL database (ChEMBL 33) [20]. A total of 2,303 entries were found, of which 502 corresponded to PAM activity data collected from four bibliographic sources [21–24]; for the sake of homogeneity of the experimental information, data from other bibliographical sources was disregarded. Only compounds with quantitative activity data against mGluR1 (EC_{50}) were kept, and manual curation was performed to eliminate duplicate molecules, and compound entries with missing or inconsistent data. The molecules were retrieved in SMILES format and standardized using the RDKIT (rdkit-pypi 2022.3.3) and MolVS 0.1.1 package (https://molvs.readthedocs.io/en/latest/).

Briefly, the largest organic fragment of the molecule (e.g., in the case of organic salts) was selected using the *fragment_parent* method, the most common isotopes of the atoms were assigned using the *isotope_parent* method, the structures were neutralized using the *charge_parent* method, and stereochemical information was removed using the MolVS *stereo_parent* method on the standardized module. The curation resulted in a data set of 169 different molecules with their EC_{50} values. Compounds with $EC_{50} \leq$ 3,000 nM were considered active (i,e, PAMs), while compounds with $EC_{50} \geq 10,000$ nM were considered inactive. Although typically, in a wet screen, an active compound at concentrations of 10,000 nM is considered a hit, given that our dataset displayed a relative abundance of active compounds at that cut-off value, we decided to set the threshold at a smaller cut-off with the expectation that the models would select more potent candidates. Molecules with EC_{50} values between 3,000 and 10,000 nM were disregarded to reduce the likelihood of mislabeling due to experimental error in the reported response value of "frontier" compounds (i.e., those near the class cutoff). The final dataset consisted of 153 molecules: 98 active compounds and 55 inactive compounds. The complete dataset can be found in the supplementary material as mGluR1_dataset.csv.

2.2 Representative Sampling

To ensure sampling of a training set with broad coverage of the chemical space occupied by the active compounds in the dataset, the in-house small molecule iterative clustering algorithm iRaPCA [25] was applied (https://github.com/Capigol/iRaPCA-v1.0), using default parameter values. iRaPCA is based on a combination of feature bagging, dimensionality reduction via Principal Component Analysis (PCA), and the k-means algorithm.

Mordred descriptor calculator (1.2.0) [26] was used to compute 1,613 conformation-independent molecular descriptors (MDs) and 100 random subsets were generated, each comprising 200 MDs. Descriptors with low variance (< 0.05) across the clustered compounds were considered uninformative and removed from the corresponding subset. The Pearson correlation coefficient was computed for every descriptor-pair in each subset; if any descriptor pair presented a correlation coefficient higher than 0.4, one of the descriptors in the pair was randomly removed. The number of principal components was restricted to two. During the k-means analysis, the k number of clusters was systematically varied between 2 and 20 to choose the data structure that, in each random subset, provided the highest Silhouette index [27]. In each iteration, the subset and k value that produce the highest Silhouette index was retained.

Finally, each resulting cluster of molecules was randomly sampled proportionally to its size to assign 55 active molecules to the training set, while the remaining 43 active compounds were randomly assigned to two test sets used for retrospective screening experiments (see Sect. 2.4). The 55 inactive compounds in the dataset were fully assigned to the training set to provide a balanced training set and prevent bias toward one class.

2.3 Molecular Descriptor Calculation, Model Generation, and Internal Validation

1,613 conformation-independent molecular descriptors were calculated for the training set using Mordred (1.2.0) [26]. Features with low variance (< 0.05) across the training set were disregarded. Feature bagging [28] was then applied to provide 3,000 random subspaces comprising 200 molecular descriptors each. A linear classifier model was obtained from each random subset, using a Forward Stepwise procedure for feature selection. Highly correlated pairs of descriptors (Pearson correlation > 0.85) were not allowed into a subset to prevent redundancy, and a maximum of ten descriptors per model was allowed to prevent overfitting. Those models that shared more than two descriptors with previous models were discarded. The scripts used for this modeling strategy can be found in the supplementary material.

The probability of spurious correlations and the robustness of the models were studied using randomization tests and leave-many-out (LMO) cross-validation. In each LMO round, random stratified subsets (containing half active compounds and half inactive compounds), composed of 20% of the total training instances, were removed. 100 LMO rounds and 100 randomization rounds were performed. In each case, the results were expressed as the mean accuracy across the 100 rounds and the corresponding standard deviation. For the LMO cross-validations, results were compared to the overall accuracy obtained for the original training set. In the case of the randomization test, the results were compared to the no model error rate value.

2.4 Retrospective Screening Experiments

The performance of the models was studied using retrospective screening experiments, in which a relatively small number of known active compounds were dispersed into a relatively large number of synthetic decoys obtained via our in-house decoy generation algorithm, LUDe (https://github.com/Capigol/LUDe_v3_test) [29]. For that, we used LUDe to generate 50 decoys per every active compound not used for training the models. We then generated two retrospective screening libraries. Retrospective Screening Library 1 (RLS1) comprised 22 active compounds and 1,100 decoys; Retrospective Screening Library 2 (RSL2) consisted of 21 active compounds and 1,050 generated decoys.

The average and early enrichment performance of the best individual models and their combinations (described in Sect. 2.5) in the retrospective screening experiments were examined through the following metrics: Area under the Receiving Operating Characteristic curve (AUROC), the Boltzmann-Enhanced Discrimination of ROC (BEDROC, $\alpha = 20$), and the enrichment factor 0.01 (EF (0.01)) [30]. The distribution of the enrichment metrics was studied using random sampling without replacement and statistically compared using the Yuen-Welch test [31]. The performance of the best individual models and the best ensemble were also examined visually using positive predictive value (PPV) surfaces [32]; the visual inspection of such surfaces was used to decide on an appropriate cutoff criterion to be used in the prospective screening experiments.

2.5 Ensemble Learning

The scores of those linear models that exhibited the higher AUROC during the first retrospective campaign (RSL1) were combined into ensemble models. To obtain these model ensembles, we used five different score combination schemes:

- MINIMUM (MIN): The minimum operator returns the lowest score among the individual scores of the combined models.
- AVERAGE (AVE): This operator returns the average of all the individual scores of the combined models.
- PRODUCT (PROD): This operator multiplies the individual scores of the combined models.
- AVERAGE RANKING (RANK): The ranking value is obtained by ordering the compounds (from 1 to the total number of compounds) according to their score in each individual model and computing the average ranking across the combined individual models.
- AVERAGE VOTING (VOT): The vote was calculated according to the equation previously used by Zhang and Muegge [33]. For each compound j, the vote for a model $votoj$ is calculated by:

Table 1. Overall accuracy of the seven best individual models on the training set and results obtained in the internal validation.

Model	Accuracy	Fisher Accuracy	LMO Accuracy
Model 256	0.873	0.490 ± 0.126	0.803 ± 0.073
Model 1446	0.782	0.485 ± 0.122	0.689 ± 0.089
Model 1117	0.827	0.488 ± 0.133	0.774 ± 0.081
Model 370	0.836	0.472 ± 0.146	0.750 ± 0.085
Model 624	0.845	0.493 ± 0.114	0.711 ± 0.092
Model 1122	0.818	0.469 ± 0.140	0.719 ± 0.086
Model 2255	0.873	0.493 ± 0.119	0.778 ± 0.081

$$votoj = max(0, integer(11 - rankj * 0.02NBD).$$

where $rankj$ indicates the ranking position taken by compound j when the compounds are ordered from best to worst in that model and NBD is the total number of compounds in the database used. The $integer$ function rounds a number down to the nearest integer. This procedure gives 10 votes for the first 2% of compounds, 9 votes for the next 2%, and so on up to 18%. Thereafter, for compounds ranked between 18–20%, only 1 vote is given. Finally, compounds ranked in the remaining 80% receive no votes. To obtain the average vote (VOT), the votes of the individual models are averaged.

2.6 Prospective Virtual Screening

The ensemble of models that showed the best values of the BEDROC metric in RSL1 was used for prospective screening of the DrugBank (5.1.11) [15], DRH [16], FoodDB (1.0) [17], and ChemTaste DB (2.0) [18, 19] databases. The leverage approach [34] was used to evaluate if the predicted compounds belonged to the applicability domain of the model (*3d/n* was used as the cutoff criterion, *d* being the number of features included in each model and *n* being the number of training set compounds). In the case of the model ensembles, the fraction of models in the ensemble for which the screened compound was within the applicability domain was calculated; in the case of the ensemble obtained via the MIN operator, it was checked that the screened compound was within the applicability domain of the model that assigned the lowest score.

3   Results

The initial search in ChEMBL for compounds with reported activity against mGluR1, one of the mGluRs downregulated in animal models of absence seizures, yielded 2,303 tested compounds. Of these, 640 were PAMs. After curation and retaining only compounds with EC_{50} s data, we obtained a final dataset consisting of 98 active compounds with EC_{50} s $\leq$ 3,000 nM and 55 inactive compounds with EC_{50} s $\geq$ 10,000 nM. From these, a balanced representative training set (55 active, 55 inactive) was obtained; to this end, active compounds were representatively sampled using the iRaPCA clustering tool. One

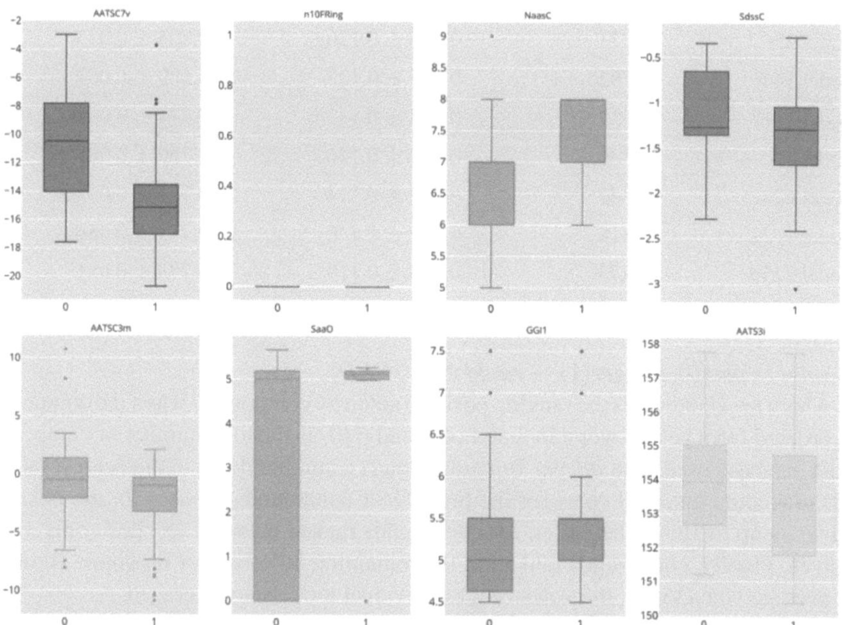

Fig. 1. Distribution of descriptor values included in Model 256 for the training set molecules. 0 represents inactive molecules and 1 represents active molecules.

of the compound clusters obtained in the first iteration of the algorithm contained 85% of the compounds, so it was subjected to successive iterations (four in total) to obtain smaller subclusters. In all cases, the Silhouette coefficient obtained was greater than 0.9, reflecting that highly cohesive and well-separated clusters were obtained.

Table 2. Descriptor value comparison for pairs of example molecules of training set.

Descriptor Name	Descriptor definition	Low value Example	Structure	High value example	Structure
AATSC7v	Averaged and centered Moreau-Broto autocorrelation of lag 7 weighted by vdW volume	-20.69 (active)		-2.97 (inactive)	
n10FRing	10-member fused ring count	0 (inactive)		1 (active)	
NaasC	Number of aromatic carbon atoms connected to two other atoms members of an aromatic ring plus an additional non-hydrogen atom.	5 (inactive)		8 (active)	
SdssC	Sum of dssC (d represents a double bond, s represents a single bond, C denotes a carbon atom)	-3.05 (active)		-0.34 (inactive)	
AATSC3m	Averaged and centered Moreau-Broto autocorrelation of lag 3 weighted by atomic mass	-14.88 (active)		10.70 (inactive)	
SaaO	Sum of aaO (a represents an atom that belongs to an aromatic ring and O denotes an oxygen atom)	0 (inactive)		5.28 (active)	
GGI1	GGI1 represents the 1-order raw topological charge	4.5 (active)		7.5 (inactive)	
AATS3i	Averaged Moreau-Broto autocorrelation of lag 3 weighted by atomic ionization potential	149.71 (active)		157.77 (inactive)	

The overall classification accuracy of all the generated models obtained was evaluated. Table 1 shows the global accuracy as well as the results obtained in the internal validation (randomization and LMO validation rounds) for the best 7 individual models (in terms of AUROC in RSL1). These models are the ones that were later combined into the best model ensemble. It can be observed that the overall accuracy range for the best individual models goes from 0.78 to 0.87. Furthermore, it is observed that the models have a low probability of arising from spurious correlations (in all cases, the average accuracy obtained in the randomization rounds was very similar to the no model error rate) and robust (the average accuracy arising from the crossed validation rounds $\pm$ 1.5 standard deviation always contains the accuracy obtained with the training set). The best individual model is shown below:

Model 256: score $= 4.591 - 0.058 * AATSC7v + 1.074 * n10FRing + 0.126 * NaasC - 0.357 * SdssC - 0.040 * AATSC3m + 0.050 * SaaO - 0.128 * GGI1 - 0.037 * AATS3i.$

Where $AATSC7v$ represents the averaged and centered Moreau-Broto autocorrelation of lag 7 weighted by van der Waals volume, $n10FRing$ is the 10-member fused ring count, $NaasC$ is the number of aromatic carbon atoms connected to two other atoms members of an aromatic ring plus an additional non-hydrogen atom, $SdssC$ codifies for the sum of $dssC$ (d represents a double bond, s represents a single bond, C denotes a carbon atom), $AATSC3m$ denotes the averaged and centered Moreau-Broto autocorrelation of lag 3 weighted by atomic mass, $SaaO$ is the sum of aaO (a, again, represents an atom that belongs to an aromatic ring and O denotes an oxygen atom), $GGI1$ represents the 1-order raw topological charge, and $AATS3i$ denotes the averaged Moreau-Broto autocorrelation of lag 3 weighted by atomic ionization potential. The distribution of the descriptor values for each class is compared in the boxplots of Fig. 1. Table 2 compares the values of each descriptor for example molecules from the training set (one from each class).

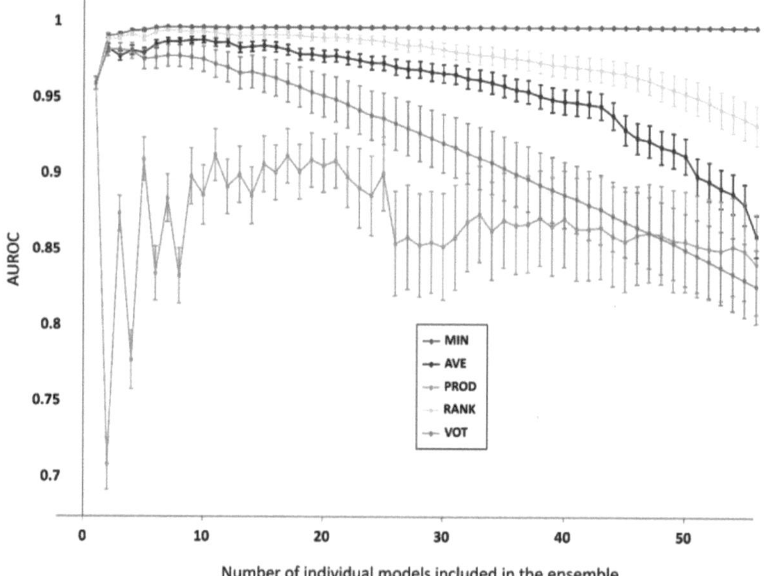

Fig. 2. AUROC vs. the number of models included in the ensemble.

Figure 2 shows the evolution of the average enrichment in the first retrospective screening versus the number of combined models. It can be observed that the MIN operator provides the best results, and that these results do not improve substantially beyond the combination of seven models. Therefore, the MIN-7 ensemble was chosen for the prospective screening. Table 3 compares the performance of the best individual model with that of the MIN-7 ensemble, in both retrospective screening experiments, in terms of average enrichment and early enrichment metrics. It is observed that in all cases the ensemble strategy was successful, achieving statistically much superior metrics ($p < 0.001$). The ensemble of seven models achieved ideal or practically ideal metrics (similar to the upper bound of the metrics) and were consistent in both retrospective experiments.

Table 3. Statistical comparison of the performance of the best individual model (Model 256) and the best model ensemble in the two retrospective screening experiments. $*p < 0.01$; $**p < 0.001$.

	Model 256	MIN 7	Model 256	MIN 7
Validation set	RSL1		RSL2	
AUC	0.962 ± 0.04	$1.000** \pm 0.000$	0.970 ± 0.04	$0.994** \pm 0.002$
BEDROC 100	0.179 ± 0.045	$0.986** \pm 0.007$	0.397 ± 0.063	$0.973** \pm 0.010$
EF (0.01)	5.890 ± 3.354	$51.000** \pm 0.0001$	19.324 ± 4.140	$50.188** \pm 0.0001$

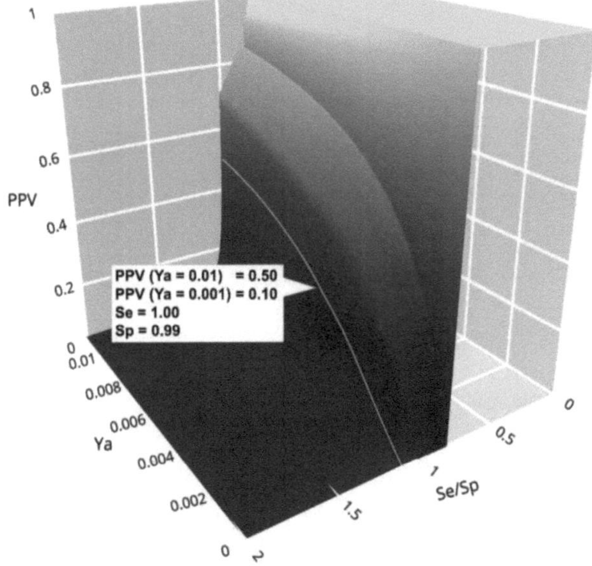

Fig. 3. PPV surface obtained when applying the MIN-7 ensemble in the first retrospective screening experiment.

Based on visual inspection of the PPV surface, we chose a MIN-7 ensemble score cutoff of 0.02, which would theoretically provide a PPV of 0.5 if the active ratio in the libraries was 0.01, and a PPV of 0.09 if the active ratio was 0.001 (Fig. 3). Since the empirical active ratio in high-throughput screening campaigns typically falls between these two values, we expect the proportion of confirmed in silico hits to be somewhere between one in two and one in ten.

Table 4. Molecular structures and general information for the six in silico hits obtained from DrugBank and the two in silico hits obtained from DRH.

Name/ DB ID	Structure	PPV (0.01)	Status	Indication(s)
Levomefolic acid (DB11256)	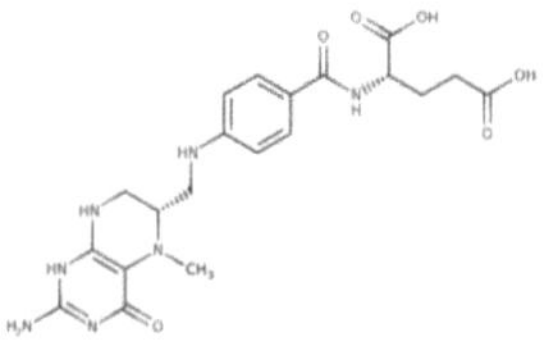	0.7710	Approved	Folate supplement used to prevent neural tube defects in pregnancy or folate deficiency
AZD-9977 (DB15418)	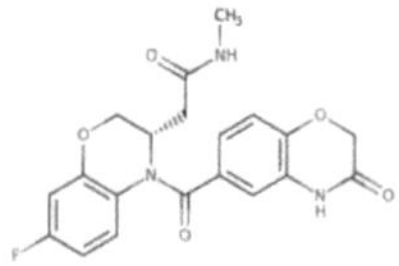	0.7261	Investigational	Cardiovascular Diseases
Chiauranib (DB16124)	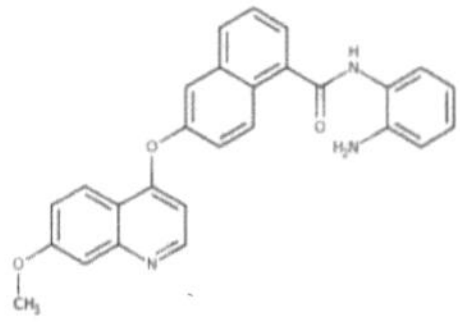	0.6897	Investigational	Different types of Cancer
Trabectedin (DB05109)	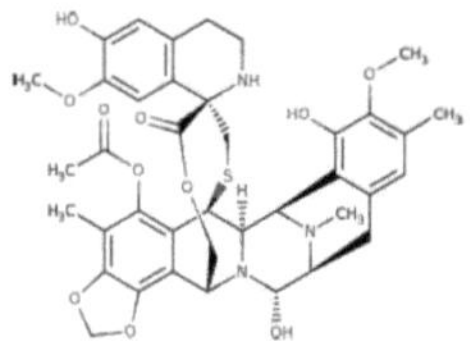	0.6493	Approved	Liposarcoma or Leiomyosarcoma
Tivozanib (DB11800)	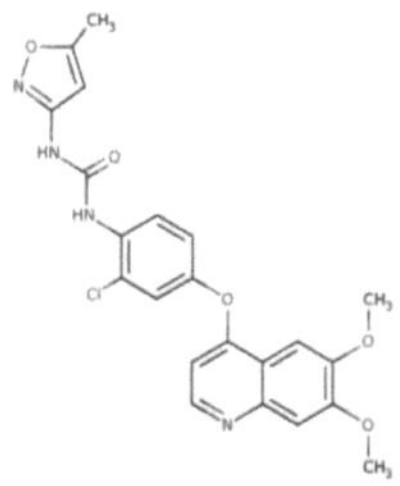	0.6135	Approved	Kidney Cancer

(continued)

Table 4. (*continued*)

Zanzalintinib (DB17525)	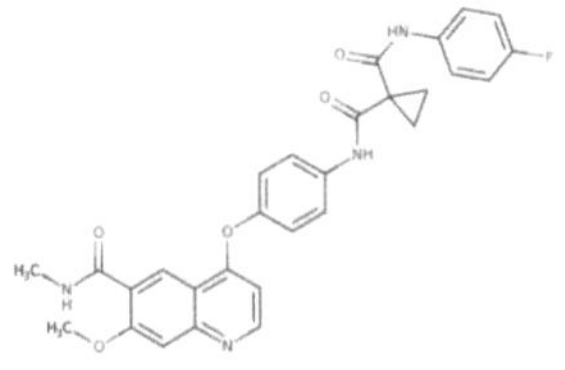	0.5814	Investigational	Different types of Cancer
GSK1562590	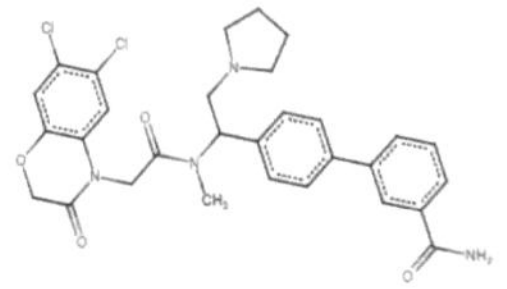	0.6896	Investigational	Urotensin receptor antagonist
W-54011	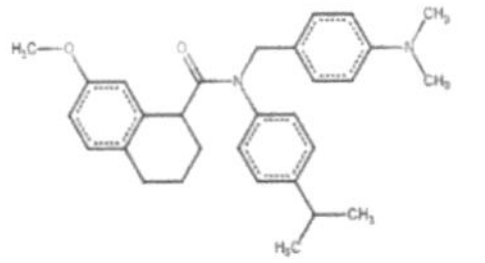	0.6134	Investigational	Anaphylatoxin chemotactic receptor antagonist

The total number of molecules screened in DrugBank, DRH, FoodDB, and Chem-TasteDB in the prospective virtual screening experiment were, respectively, 11,800, 6,798, 70,000, and 4,075. The number of in silico hits (i.e., molecules predicted as mGluR1 PAMs) obtained from them was 29, 19, 283, and 22, in that order and regard?less of the domain of applicability, and 6, 5, 110, and 5, in that order and considering the domain of applicability. Three out of five final in silico hits obtained from DRH were also obtained from DrugBank.. Interestingly, the in silico hit rate coincides with the order of empirical high throuput screening rates observed in high-throughput wet screening campaigns, which would suggest a relatively low false positive rate. The molecular structures and additional information of the six hits obtained from DrugBank and the two hits from DRH (repositioning hits and therefore the most direct candidates in terms of translatability potential) are shown in Table 4.

4 Discussion and Conclusions

We have developed meta-classifiers capable of identifying compounds that modulate subtype 1 metabotropic glutamate receptors. The best meta-classifier achieved excellent enrichment metric values (ideal or near-ideal) in two independent retrospective screening experiments. After validation, this ensemble was applied in a retrospective screening campaign of fout databases, aiming to detect repositioned compounds and food contistituents with potential modulatory activity on the chosen target. In particular, the identification of eight repositioning candidates stands out. However, it should be noted that not all of these repositioning candidates are equally promising, particularly considering their ADMET properties. Taking into account that we are searching for central nervous system therapeutics, it is relevant that candidates have good blood–brain barrier (BBB) permeability. We have predicted the BBB permeability using DeepPK, and two in silico hits, W-54011 and Trabectedin, were predicted to be non-permeable [35]. On the other hand, Trabectedin is a DNA-alkylating agent with a poor safety profile. Future studies should focus on molecular docking and dynamics studies of the most suitable candidates and subsequent experimental validation of the most promising candidates.

Acknowledgments. This study was funded by Agencia I+D+i (grant number PICT 2019–1075). All authors are members of UNLP. LNA and AT are members of the Argentinean National Council of Scientific and Technical Research (CONICET). MJF is a doctoral fellow of CONICET.

References

1. Niswender, C.M., Conn, P.J.: Metabotropic glutamate receptors: physiology, pharmacology, and disease. Ann. Rev. Pharmacol. Toxicol. **50**, 295–322 (2010)
2. Mercier, M.S., Lodge, D.: Group III metabotropic glutamate receptors: pharmacology, physiology and therapeutic potential. Neurochem. Res. **39**, 1876–1894 (2014)
3. Luessen, D.J., Conn, P.J.: Allosteric modulators of metabotropic glutamate receptors as novel therapeutics for neuropsychiatric disease. Pharmacol. Rev. **74**(3), 630–661 (2022)
4. Strauss, A., et al.: Structural basis of positive allosteric modulation of metabotropic glutamate receptor activation and internalization. Nat. Commun. **15**(1), 6498 (2024)
5. Alexander, G.M., Godwin, D.W.: Metabotropic glutamate receptors as a strategic target for the treatment of epilepsy. Epilepsy Res. **71**(1), 1–22 (2006)
6. Celli, R., Santolini, I., Van Luijtelaar, G., Ngomba, R.T., Bruno, V., Nicoletti, F.: Targeting metabotropic glutamate receptors in the treatment of epilepsy: rationale and current status. Expert Opin. Ther. Targets **23**(4), 341–351 (2019)
7. Cellim, R., et al.: Pharmacological activation of mGlu5 receptors with the positive allosteric modulator VU0360172, modulates thalamic GABAergic transmission. Neuropharmacology **178**, 108240 (2020)
8. Talevi, A., Enrique, A.V., Bruno-Blanch, L.E.: Anticonvulsant activity of artificial sweeteners: a structural link between sweet-taste receptor T1R3 and brain glutamate receptors. Bioorg. Med. Chem. Lett. **22**(12), 4072–4074 (2012)

9. Di Ianni, M.E., et al.: Is there a relationship between sweet taste and seizures? Anticonvulsant and proconvulsant effects of non-nutritive sweeteners. Comb. Chem. High Throughput Screen. **18**(4), 335–345 (2015)

10. Di Ianni, M.E., et al.: Computer-aided identification of anticonvulsant effect of natural nonnutritive sweeteners stevioside and rebaudioside A. Assay Drug Dev. Technol. **13**(6), 313–318

11. Jiang, P., et al.: Identification of the cyclamate interaction site within the transmembrane domain of the human sweet taste receptor subunit T1R3. J. Biol. Chem. **280**(40), 34296–34305 (2005)

12. Cong, X., Chéron, J.B., Golebiowski, J., Antonczak, S., Fiorucci, S.: Allosteric modulation mechanism of the mGluR5 transmembrane domain. J. Chem. Inf. Model. **59**(6), 2871–2878 (2019)

13. Strauss, A., et al.: Structural basis of allosteric modulation of metabotropic glutamate receptor activation and desensitization. Nat. Commun. **15**(1), 6498 (2024)

14. Leonti, M., Baker, J., Staub, P., Casu, L., Hawkins, J.: Taste shaped the use of botanical drugs. Elife **12**, RP90070 (2024)

15. Knox, C., et al.: DrugBank 6.0: the DrugBank knowledgebase for 2024. Nucleic Acids Res. **52**(D1), D1265–D1275 (2024)

16. Corsello, S.M., et al.: The drug repurposing hub: a next-generation drug library and information resource. Nat. Med. **23**(4), 405–408 (2017)

17. Harrington, R.A., Adhikari, V., Rayner, M., Scarborough, P.: Nutrient composition databases in the age of big data: foodDB, a comprehensive, real-time database infrastructure. BMJ Open **9**(6), e026652 (2019)

18. Rojas, C., Ballabio, D., Pacheco Sarmiento, K., Pacheco Jaramillo, E., Mendoza, M., García, F.: ChemTastesDB: a curated database of molecular tastants. Food Chem Mol Sci **4**, 100090 (2022)

19. Rojas, C., Abril-González, M., Ballabio, D., García, F.: ChemTastesPredictor: an ensemble of machine learning classifiers to predict the taste of molecular tastants. Chemom. Intell. Lab. Syst. **261**, 105380 (2025)

20. Zdrazil, B., et al.: The ChEMBL Database in 2023: a drug discovery platform spanning multiple bioactivity data types and time periods. Nucleic Acids Res. **52**(D1), D1180–D1192 (2024)

21. Garcia-Barrantes, P.M., Cho, H.P., Blobaum, A.L., Niswender, C.M., Conn, P.J., Lindsley, C.W.: Lead optimization of the VU0486321 series of mGlu1 PAMs. Part 1: SAR of modifications to the central aryl core. Bioorg. Med. Chem. Lett. **25**(22), 5107–5110 (2015)

22. Garcia-Barrantes, P.M., et al.: Lead optimization of the VU0486321 series of mGlu(1) PAMs. part 2: SAR of alternative 3-methyl heterocycles and progress towards an in vivo tool. Bioorg. Med. Chem. Lett. **26**(3), 751–756 (2016)

23. Garcia-Barrantes, P.M., Cho, H.P., Blobaum, A.L., Niswender, C.M., Conn, P.J., Lindsley, C.W. Lead optimization of the VU0486321 series of mGlu1 PAMs. part 3. engineering plasma stability by discovery and optimization of isoindolinone analogs. Bioorg. Med. Chem. Lett. **26**(8), 1869–1872 (2016)

24. Garcia-Barrantes, P.M., et al.: Development of novel, CNS penetrant positive allosteric modulators for the metabotropic glutamate receptor subtype 1 (mGlu1), based on an N-(3-Chloro-4-(1,3-dioxoisoindolin-2-yl)phenyl)-3-methylfuran-2-carboxamide scaffold, that potentiate wild type and mutant mGlu1 receptors found in schizophrenics. J. Med. Chem. **58**(20), 7959–7971 (2015)

25. Prada Gori, D.N., Llanos, M.A., Bellera, C.L., Talevi, A., Alberca, L.N.: IRaPCA and SOMoC: development and validation of web applications for new approaches for the clustering of small molecules. J. Chem. Inf. Model. **62**(12), 2987–2998 (2022)

26. Moriwaki, H., Tian, Y.S., Kawashita, N., Takagi, T.: Mordred: a molecular descriptor calculator. J Cheminform **10**, 4 (2018)
27. Rousseeuw, P.J.: Silhouettes: a graphical aid to the interpretation and validation of cluster analysis. J. Comput. Appl. Math. **20**, 53–65 (1987)
28. Ho, T.K.: The random subspace method for constructing decision forests. IEEE Trans. Pattern Anal. Mach. Intell. **20**(8), 832–844 (1998)
29. Alberca, L.N., Prada Gori, D.N., Fallico, M.J., Fassio, A.V., Talevi, A., Bellera, C.L.: LIDEB's Useful Decoys (LUDe): A freely available decoy-generation tool. Benchmarking and scope. Artif. Intell. Life Sci. **7**, 100129 (2025)
30. Truchon, J.-F., Bayly, C.I.: Evaluating virtual screening methods: good and bad metrics for the "early recognition" problem. J. Chem. Inf. Model. **47**(2), 488–508 (2007)
31. Welch, B.L.: The generalization of "Student's" problem when several different population variances are involved". Biometrika **34**(1–2), 28–35 (1947)
32. Morales, J.F., et al.: Positive predictive value surfaces as a complementary tool to assess the performance of virtual screening methods. Mini-Rev. Med. Chem. **20**(14), 1447–1460 (2020)
33. Zhang, Q., Muegge, I.: Scaffold hopping through virtual screening using 2D and 3D similarity descriptors: ranking, voting, and consensus scoring. J. Med. Chem. **49**(5), 1536–1548 (2006)
34. Yasri, A., Hartsough, D.: Toward an optimal procedure for variable selection and QSAR model building. J. Chem. Inf. Comput. Sci. **41**(5), 1218–1227 (2001)
35. Myung, Y., de Sá, A.G.C., Ascher, D.B.: Deep-PK: deep learning for small molecule pharmacokinetic and toxicity prediction. Nucleic Acids Res. **52**(W1), W469–W475 (2024)

A Comparative Analysis of ANN, TabNet and FT-Transformer Models in EEG Classification of Neuropsychiatric Disorders

Mateus Balda Mota[2] , Alessandro Bof de Oliveira[1] , Patricia Bof[1] , and Dante Augusto Couto Barone[2(✉)]

[1] LAPIA, UNIPAMPA, Alegrete, RS 97.541-300, Brazil
alessandrobof@unipampa.edu.br
[2] Instituto de Informática, UFRGS, CP 15.064, Porto 91.501-970, Brazil
barone@inf.ufrgs.br
https://sites.unipampa.edu.br/lapia/

Abstract. Neuropsychiatric disorders constitute a substantial global health burden, affecting approximately 970 million individuals worldwide, with a exacerbation during the COVID-19 pandemic. This investigation presents a comparative analysis of three state-of-the-art artificial intelligence architectures–Multilayer Perceptron (ANN), TabNet, and FT-Transformer–for the automated classification of neuropsychiatric disorders using electroencephalographic (EEG) signals. The study employed a clinically validated dataset comprising 945 participants stratified across seven diagnostic categories: mood disorders, addictive disorders, trauma and stress-related disorders, schizophrenia, anxiety disorders, healthy controls, and obsessive-compulsive disorder. The neurophysiological data, already pre-processed in a previous study, were used in conjunction with the Synthetic Minority Over-sampling Technique (SMOTE) due to class imbalance. The dataset has the features: power spectral density (PSD) for six frequency bands, functional connectivity (FC), age, sex, and intelligence quotient (IQ). Experimental results demonstrated TabNet's superior generalization capability across multiple psychiatric disorders, achieving notable performance in mood disorders (93.50% accuracy) and addictive disorders (96.00% accuracy). Our proposed ANN architecture exhibited exceptional discriminative power for schizophrenia classification (94.38% AUC) and obsessive-compulsive disorder detection (98.89% AUC). The FT-Transformer model yielded competitive performance, particularly in anxiety disorder identification. These findings underscore the critical importance of disorder-specific model selection and feature engineering, advancing the development of robust computational frameworks for neuropsychiatric diagnostic support systems.

Keywords: Neuropsychiatric classification · EEG · Artificial Intelligence models

1   Introduction

Neuropsychiatric disorders directly impact social life and productivity. In 2019, it was estimated that 1 in 8 people worldwide lived with a mental disorder, totaling 970 million [20]. This number increased significantly with the COVID-19 pandemic, with a 26% rise in anxiety cases and a 28% rise in depression cases within just one year [20].

The classification by an expert, using the DSM-5 (Diagnostic and Statistical Manual of Mental Disorders, 5th Edition) criteria, often relies on evaluating behavioral symptoms and subjective reports, which can result in inaccurate or inconsistent diagnoses [3].

Considering this issue, methods for evaluating and diagnosing neuropsychiatric disorders are becoming increasingly important. Among the tools available, the electroencephalogram (EEG) stands out for its ability to provide data on brain activity across different regions of the brain [18], making it valuable for identifying mental disorders [4]. When combined with machine learning approaches, the use of EEG has demonstrated relevant accuracy, particularly in disorders such as depression, schizophrenia, and anxiety [1,5,11,13,14].

In this work, we propose a method based on a deep neural network to classify EEGs and compare it to two other models: TabNet [2] and FTTransformer [8]. These methods were chosen due to their capacity to handle tabular data as well as transforming the data representation. Another important contribution of this work is handling the unbalanced number of data samples in each class and determining which features of the dataset are more relevant in the classification task.

In Sect. 3, we describe the dataset, the preprocessing methods, and the metrics used to analyse the performance of the models; in Sect. 4 we present our proposed method (ANN) and the comparative models; in Sect. 5, we show the experimental results, and the conclusion and future works are in Sect. 6.

2   Related Works

Artificial neural networks have been demonstrated to be powerful tools in analyzing EEG signals [1,4], and [10], especially in neuropsychiatric contexts. They can classify complex data, surpassing conventional methods in terms of accuracy, improving the diagnosis of conditions such as mental disorders [14].

According to AHmed et al. [1] and Baldo [10], deep neural networks have demonstrated good performance in diagnostic classification, outperforming other machine learning methods. For example, Wang et al. [19] has used a MUCHf-Net neural network to classify EEGs from individuals with depression (DP), schizophrenia (SCZ), and healthy controls. The results showed that the network achieved an accuracy of 0.9112 in distinguishing between control and pathological EEGs, with the greatest contribution from the low-frequency bands and the frontal and parietal regions of the brain. The analysis also indicated that the model had more difficulty differentiating between DP and SCZ.

The work of Shah et al. [17] categorized individuals with schizophrenia (SZ), biological relatives (REL), and healthy controls (HC) using resting EEG signals from 78 cortical regions. The proposed deep neural network ETSNet achieved an accuracy of 0.9957 for classifying SZ, REL, and HC with open eyes (EO), and 0.9315 for closed eyes (EC). The authors in paper [1], used EEG and deep learning models (ANN, KNN, LSTM, Bi-LSTM, CNN-LSTM). The ANN achieved an accuracy of 0.9683 in identifying obsessive-compulsive disorder using all frequency bands. The CNN-LSTM model achieved the same accuracy rate for adjustment disorder. The KNN and LSTM models reached an accuracy of 0.9894 for acute stress disorder with specific features, while KNN and Bi-LSTM achieved an accuracy of 0.9788 for obsessive-compulsive disorder.

3   Methodology

The Sect. 3.1 describes the EEG dataset, Sect. 3.2 describes the preprocessing steps to prepare the dataset. The metric used to evaluate the experiments are show in Sect. 3.3 and finally our proposed model, TabNet and FTTransformer, are described in Sect. 4.

3.1   EEG Dataset

We have used the dataset presented by Park et al. [12], where the data were collected from SMG-SNU Boramae Medical Center, and confirmation of the diagnosis was established by two psychiatrists and two psychologists between March 2019 and August 2019. The dataset has samples of 945 patients aged between 18 and 70 years, with a mean age of 30.59 ± 11.78, an average education level of 13.43 ± 2.55 years, and an average IQ of 101.58 ± 17.02. The primary disorder categories consist of 7 classes, with a number of samples: mood disorder = 266, addictive disorder = 186, trauma and stress-related disorder = 128, schizophrenia = 117, anxiety disorder = 107, healthy control = 95, and obsessive-compulsive disorder = 46. Data collection used 19 EEG channels based on the international 10–20 system. The data were pre-processed by [13] using the Fast Fourier Transform (FFT) to convert the signals into the frequency domain. The Power Spectral Density (PSD) was calculated for the following frequency bands: delta 1 to 4 Hz, theta 4 to 8 Hz, alpha 8 to 12 Hz, beta 12 to 25 Hz, high beta 25 to 30 Hz), and gamma 30 to 40 Hz, providing the signal power in each band. Functional Coherence (FC) was used to evaluate the synchronization between different brain regions. The detailed method is described in [13]. After that, we have 1140 features (114 PSD and 1026 FC) and three quantitative variables (age, education, and IQ). The data was randomly divided into training, validation, and test sets with proportions of 70%, 15%, and 15%, respectively. The training set was used to fine-tune the model, while the validation set was used to perform model predictions during each training epoch. Finally, after the training phase, the test set was used to calculate the model's evaluation metrics.

3.2   Preprocessing Data

Samples with missing values (*NaN*) were identified (28 samples) for the features *education* and *IQ*. To impute the *NaN* values, we use the method *KNNImputer* [15] with the number of neighbors set to 5 that demonstrated the best results. Due to the unbalanced number of samples in each class, we have used the method SMOTE (Synthetic Minority Oversampling Technique) [7] to generate synthetic samples and standardize the number of samples to 266 (the number of samples in the largest class). The SMOTE method was used because it achieves good results with low computational cost, mitigating biased data caused by class imbalance. After that, we normalized the features using the *z-score* method. The Smote method was used only in training stage.

After balancing, the dataset was divided into subsets based on three groups of attributes: PSD, FC, and PSD + FC. All sets include the features age, education and IQ. Each group was individually combined with six frequency bands (delta, theta, alpha, beta, high beta, and gamma) and also with all bands combined, resulting in 21 combinations per disorder.

3.3   Metrics for Performance Evaluation

The metrics used in this work to evaluate the performance of the classification models were *Accurary* (Eq. 1) as defined by [6] and detailed below:

$$Accuracy = \frac{TP + TN}{TP + TN + FP + FN},\tag{1}$$

where TP is True Positive, i.e. when the patient is correctly classified as having the disorder and TN is True Negative, when the patient is classified correctly as a control group. The FP and FN are False Positive, and False Negative, respectively, and are used when the patients are misclassified. The other metric used is AUC that represents the area under the ROC curve. The AUC evaluates the quality of a model's predictions by measuring the area under the Receiver Operating Characteristic (ROC) curve, which plots the True Positive (TP) against the False Positive (FP) at different classification thresholds. An AUC of 1.0 represents a perfect classifier, while an AUC of 0.5 represents a model no better than random guessing in a binary classification problem.

4   Artificial Intelligence Models

In this section, we will introduce our proposed deep artificial neural network model of the Multilayer Perceptron 4.1. In the subsequent sections, we will briefly describe the TabNet 4.2 and FTTransformer 4.3 models.

4.1 Proposed Artificial Neural Network Model

The neural network architecture [9] and [16] consists of an input layer followed by four hidden layers, with a number of neurons defined by the list (1024, 512, 256, 128, 64), and an output layer of dimension 2 for FC and PSD+FC sets and (128, 64, 32, 16) and output 2 for PSD set. Each hidden layer is followed by *Batch Normalization - BatchNorm1d* and the GELU (*Gaussian Error Linear Unit*) activation function. A *dropout* of 10% is applied after each hidden layer to prevent *overfitting*. The loss function chosen was Cross Entropy Loss with optimizer sets up to Adam. The learning rate scheduler used was *Reduce Plateau*, which reduces the learning rate by 10% if the loss does not improve after 3 epochs, with a minimum learning rate of (1×10^{-6}). The model was developed using the programming language *Python*[1] 3.13.7 and the libraries *PyTorch*[2] 2.8 and *Scikit-Learn*[3] 1.7.

4.2 TabNet Model

TabNet is a neural network model specifically designed for tabular data, as proposed by [2]. It employs a sequential attention-based architecture capable of supervised or self-supervised learning, allowing the model to select which features to consider. This structure enhances the robustness and accuracy of the model by choosing the most relevant features for the prediction. TabNet also incorporates information compression mechanisms and induced sparsity, contributing to improved computational efficiency and generalization capability.

The training was conducted using the Adam optimizer, recognized for its efficiency in handling high-dimensional problems and noisy data. Additionally, a learning rate scheduler was employed with a step size parameter of 30 and a gamma of 0.9, implying a 10% reduction in the learning rate every 30 epochs, thereby promoting stable model convergence. The implementation of the TabNet[4] model, version 4.1.0, was developed with *Pytorch*.

4.3 FTTranformer Model

The FTTransformer (*Feature Tokenizer Transformer*) is a variation of Transformer-based models developed to handle tabular data, as proposed by [8]. It combines feature tokenization with the multi-head self-attention blocks. The model handles each feature as an independent token, where the FT-Transformer effectively models complex interactions among variables. The use of embeddings and normalized layers facilitates stable training on high-dimensional datasets, such as those derived from biomedical or neurophysiological signals.

The model was configured to accept only numerical inputs, and the number of input features was set according to the number of columns in the training dataset.

---

[1] https://www.python.org/.
[2] https://pytorch.org/.
[3] https://scikit-learn.org/stable/.
[4] https://pypi.org/project/pytorch-tabnet/.

For the binary classification task, the output was defined as a single neuron. Additionally, the parameter output relies exclusively on the transformer's last token, as recommended for classification tasks. The FTTransformer[5] model used was the version 1.1.1 was developed with *Pytorch*.

5   Experimental Results

In this section, we show the experimental results using the different models on the test set. In Table 1, we have used all features of the test set. In the column Model, we have the best model for the disorders. The TabNet model achieved the best results for mood disorders (93.50% accuracy and 0.93 AUC) and trauma and stress-related disorders (0.89 AUC), whereas the ANN has excellent results in schizophrenia (0.94 AUC) and addictive disorder (0.92 AUC). The FT-Transformer demonstrated significant performance in anxiety disorder (76.70% accuracy) and obsessive-compulsive disorder (0.87 AUC). These results suggest that the choice of model and extracted features (PSD and FC) significantly impact performance, with TabNet being particularly effective in generalizing across classes.

Table 1. Performance of the methods TabNet, ANN, and FTTransformer for different disorders using all features. Highest overall accuracy of the models. ACC = Accuracy; AUC = Area under the ROC Curve.

Disorder type	Disorder	Model	ACC(%)	AUC
Main disorder	Addictive	ANN	84.00	0.92
	Anxiety	FTTransformer	76.70	0.72
	Mood	TabNet	93.50	0.93
	Obsessive compulsive	FTTransformer	84.20	0.87
	Schizophrenia	ANN	87.20	0.94
	Trauma and stress	TabNet	86.50	0.89

The Fig. 1 displays the accuracy and AUC values corresponding to the highest accuracies and AUC achieved for each disorder. In terms of accuracy, the TabNet model presents better overall results, while our proposed artificial neural network reaches the best overall performance in the AUC metric. The Table 2 summarizes the performance of the three models: ANN, FTTransformer, and TabNet models using the test set, and shows the results for healthy controls versus mental disorders. The best feature configuration (PSD and FC) and EEG band for each disorder is indicated. The TabNet demonstrated the highest performance in four out of six disorders, notably excelling in addictive disorders with 96.00% accuracy and 0.95 AUC, as well as in schizophrenia with 91.49% accuracy and 0.95

---

[5] https://pypi.org/project/pytorch-tabular/.

AUC. ANN achieved superior results in obsessive-compulsive disorder, attaining 92.11% accuracy and 98.89% AUC, and also performed strongly in trauma- and stress-related disorders with 94.23% accuracy and 0.97 AUC. For mood disorders, TabNet achieved 97.20% accuracy, while ANN obtained the highest AUC at 0.99. In anxiety disorders, TabNet outperformed the other models with 90.70% accuracy, while ANN demonstrated competitive AUC at 0.85. The best feature configurations varied across models, with Beta PSD + FC and Delta PSD frequently contributing to the optimal results.

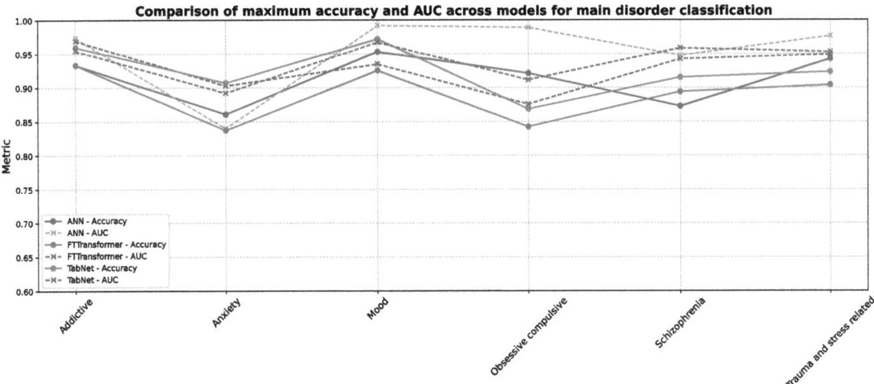

Fig. 1. Comparison of the maximum accuracy and AUC among the models for the classification of disorders.

Table 2. Model performance in classifying healthy controls vs. disorders, based on the best feature configuration for each disorder. Metrics refer to the best set of features (Best feat.) per disorder. AUC = area under the ROC curve; FC = functional connectivity; PSD = power spectral density.

Disorder	Best feat.	Accuracy(%)			AUC		
		ANN	FTT	TabNet	ANN	FTT	TabNet
Addictive	Beta PSD + FC	84.00	78.67	**96.00**	0.92	0.80	**0.95**
Anxiety	Delta PSD	79.07	76.74	**90.70**	0.85	0.85	**0.89**
Mood	Beta PSD + FC	95.33	87.85	**97.20**	**0.99**	0.93	0.96
Ob. compulsive	Delta PSD	**92.11**	81.58	76.32	**0.98**	0.87	0.75
Schizophrenia	Beta PSD	80.85	87.23	**91.49**	0.86	0.93	**0.95**
Trauma and stress	Whole PSD	**94.23**	90.38	88.46	**0.97**	0.94	0.93

6   Conclusions

In this work, we proposed a comparative analysis of three neural network models: our proposed Multilayer Perceptron (ANN), TabNet, and FT-Transformer, for the binary classification of neuropsychiatric disorders using electroencephalographic (EEG) signals. We utilized a set of features, including power spectral density (PSD), functional connectivity (FC), age, sex, and IQ. Our experimental results demonstrated superior performance with average accuracies of 93.62% compared to prior works, significantly surpassing multiclass classification accuracies of 60–80% reported in other studies. TabNet model consistently exhibited superior generalization capabilities across multiple psychiatric disorders, achieving 97.20% accuracy in mood disorders and 96.00% accuracy with a 0.95 AUC for addictive disorders. It also showed robust performance in schizophrenia with 91.49% accuracy and a 0.95 AUC, and 90.70% accuracy for anxiety disorders. Our proposed ANN model demonstrated exceptional discriminative power in specific conditions, reaching 92.11% accuracy and an outstanding 0.98 AUC for obsessive-compulsive disorder. Furthermore, ANN reached 94.23% accuracy and a 0.97 AUC for trauma and stress-related disorders, and the highest AUC of 0.99 for mood disorders. The FT-Transformer model, while competitive, notably achieved 76.70% accuracy for anxiety disorder identification. These findings critically show the importance of disorder-specific model selection and the effective integration of domain-specific feature representations, such as PSD and FC, to advance robust diagnostic support systems for neuropsychiatric conditions.

In future work, we intend to explore more artificial intelligence models and create synthetic data using generative adversarial networks. The results obtained in this work encourage us to develop an ANN ensemble model.

Acknowledgments. We would like to thanks to [12] to make available the EEG dataset.

Disclosure of Interests. The authors have no competing interests to declare that are relevant to the content of this article.

References

1. Ahmed, Z., Wali, A., Shahid, S., Zikria, S., Rasheed, J., Asuroglu, T.: Psychiatric disorders from eeg signals through deep learning models. IBRO Neurosci. Rep. (2024)
2. Arik, S.Ö., Pfister, T.: Tabnet: attentive interpretable tabular learning. In: Proceedings of the AAAI Conference on Artificial Intelligence, vol. 35, pp. 6679–6687 (2021)
3. Association, A.P.: Diagnostic and Statistical Manual of Mental Disorders: DSM-5, vol. 5. American Psychiatric Association (2013)
4. Ay, B., et al.: Automated depression detection using deep representation and sequence learning with eeg signals. J. Med. Syst. **43**, 1–12 (2019)

5. Beniczky, S., Schomer, D.L.: Electroencephalography: basic biophysical and technological aspects important for clinical applications. Epileptic Disorders **22**, 697–715 (2020)
6. Brownlee, J.: Tour of evaluation metrics for imbalanced classification (2021). https://machinelearningmastery.com/tour-of-evaluation-metrics-for-imbalanced-classification/, acessado em: 27 nov. 2024
7. Chawla, N.V., Bowyer, K.W., Hall, L.O., Kegelmeyer, W.P.: Smote: synthetic minority over-sampling technique. J. Artif. Intell. Res. **16**, 321–357 (2002)
8. Gorishniy, Y., Rubachev, I., Khrulkov, V., Babenko, A.: Revisiting deep learning models for tabular data. Adv. Neural. Inf. Process. Syst. **34**, 18932–18943 (2021)
9. Haykin, S.: Neural networks: principles and practice. Bookman **11**(900) (2011)
10. Júnior, S.B.: Algoritmos genéticos e aprendizado profundo baseado em redes neurais recorrentes do tipo LSTM para auxílio ao diagnóstico médico. Ph.D. thesis, Universidade de São Paulo (2023)
11. Müller-Putz, G.R.: Electroencephalography. Handbook Clin. Neurol. **168**, 249–262 (2020)
12. Park, S.M.: Eeg machine learning (2021), Accessed 16 August 2021. https://osf.io/8bsvr
13. Park, S.M., et al.: Identification of major psychiatric disorders from resting-state electroencephalography using a machine learning approach. Front. Psychiatry **12**, 707581 (2021)
14. Parsa, M., et al.: Eeg-based classification of individuals with neuropsychiatric disorders using deep neural networks: a systematic review of current status and future directions. Comput. Methods Programs Biomed. **240**, 107683 (2023)
15. Pedregosa, F., et al.: Scikit-learn: machine learning in python. J. Mach. Learn. Res. **12**, 2825–2830 (2011)
16. Russell, S.J., Norvig, P.: Artificial Intelligence: A Modern Approach. Pearson (2022)
17. Shah, S.J.H., Albishri, A., Kang, S.S., Lee, Y., Sponheim, S.R., Shim, M.: Etsnet: a deep neural network for eeg-based temporal-spatial pattern recognition in psychiatric disorder and emotional distress classification. Comput. Biol. Med. **158**, 106857 (2023)
18. Siuly, S., Li, Y., Zhang, Y.: Eeg signal analysis and classification. IEEE Trans. Neural Syst. Rehabil. Eng. **11**, 141–144 (2016)
19. Wang, Z., et al.: Automated rest eeg-based diagnosis of depression and schizophrenia using a deep convolutional neural network. IEEE Access **10**, 104472–104485 (2022)
20. World Health Organization: Mental disorders, June 2022. https://www.who.int/news-room/fact-sheets/detail/mental-disorders, Accessed 10 Oct 2024

Computational and Experimental Approaches for the Discovery of New Anticonvulsant Drugs

Santiago Matias Ruatta, Mateo Girardi, Alan Talevi, Luciana Gavernet, and Melisa Edith Gantner[✉]

Laboratory of Bioactive Compounds Research and Development (LIDeB), Faculty of Exact Sciences, National University of La Plata (UNLP), 47 and 115, B1900AKN, La Plata, Buenos Aires, Argentina
mgantner@biol.unlp.edu.ar

Abstract. Two compounds that share the benzylsulfamide scaffold were proposed as carbonic anhydrase (CA) inhibitors by docking simulations. This computational approach was used to better understand the binding interactions between these structures and the hCAVII isoform, a non-conventional target for antiseizure medications. Our results revealed a common binding mode between the sulfamide function and the active site, but two different orientations for the aryl group, depending on the compound analyzed. The two compounds designed using structure-based approximations were synthesized for further biological evaluation.

Keywords: Epilepsy · Carbonic Anhydrase · Sulfamides · Docking · hCAVII · Computer-aided Drug Design

1 Introduction

Epilepsy is one of the most frequent neurological diseases. It affects about 50 million people worldwide and this number is expected to rise further considering the increasing life expectancy [1].

Additionally, there is an increasing ratio of people that survive conditions that lead to epilepsy, such as birth trauma, traumatic brain injury, infections of the brain, and stroke [1].

The disease is characterized by spontaneous repetitive seizures (with observable or unobservable manifestations) and their classification is subject to constant revision, since the therapeutic solutions vary according to different seizure types and epileptic syndromes [2]. People with epilepsy experience a higher risk of premature death than the general population, especially in low and middle income countries [1]. In addition, seizures can cause physical problems (such as fractures and injuries) and are associated with comorbid neuropsychiatric conditions (such as anxiety or depression) [1].

Antiseizure drugs (ASD) are the first-line therapy for epilepsy. As a general rule, they have the objective to restore the fine balance in the neuronal activity. In terms of their mechanism of action at therapeutic concentrations, most ASD act as voltage-gated sodium channels blockers, interact with GABA-related targets, block calcium channels

A. Talevi and V. Rosa Cota (Eds.): LAWCN 2025, CCIS 2734, pp. 46–54, 2026.
https://doi.org/10.1007/978-3-032-14664-9_5

and/or interfere with the glutamate transmission [3, 4]. Among other less explored mechanisms, the Carbonic Anhydrase (CA) enzyme has been studied as a molecular target of ASD [4], with known approved ASDs, such as topiramate, partially acting via CA inhibition. The twelve catalytically active human isoforms of this metalloenzyme catalyze the reversible hydration reaction between CO_2 and HCO_3^-, and the equilibrium between these species influences the pH regulation of the intracellular and extracellular spaces [5]. Changes in brain pH influence neuronal excitability, affecting the generation, progression, and severity of seizures. In this scenario, the human isoform CAVII (hCAVII), mainly expressed in neurons of the cortex, hippocampus, and thalamus, represents an interesting molecular target for new ASDs. This isoform appears to play a role in the generation of seizures by increasing depolarizing and excitatory GABAergic transmission driven by HCO_3^- as a consequence of an intense activation of the GABAA receptor [4].

Most CA inhibitors are small molecules that exert their action by interactions with the catalytic center, using a zinc binding function (ZBF) to physically block the entrance/exit of substrates. This center is located at the bottom of a half hydrophobic and half hydrophilic cavity of the enzyme, and is composed by a zinc atom tetrahedrally coordinated with three histidine residues through one nitrogen atom of the imidazole rings [6]. The sulfonamide group ($R-SO_2-NH-$) is the classical ZBF, coordinating with the fourth site of coordination though the deprotonated N atom, while the O atoms interact with conserved amino acids in the active site [6].

In previous investigations we have explored compounds with the sulfamide functionality ($-NH-SO_2-NH-$) as hCAVII inhibitors. We found that the "extra" N atom of sulfamides relative to sulfonamides promotes new interactions with the active site [7]. Additionally, we found that sometimes the N, N'-disubstitution provides isoform selectivity, yielding compounds with higher potency in hCAVII (the ASD target) relative to the ubiquitous hCAII isoform, from which the inhibition can lead to adverse effects [4, 7, 8]. Based on molecular dynamics simulations we proposed that the origin of selectivity could be partially attributed to the capacity of the hCAVII cleft to accommodate more "elongated" inhibitors, in comparison with the active site in hCAII [7]. Additionally, the hydrophilic region near the active site includes the distinctive Gln69 and Lys93 residues in hCAVII (Asn67 and Ile91 in hCAII), which could influence the differences in the size and shape of the active site, as well as in the interactions with ligands [7].

In this investigation we performed molecular docking simulations in order to propose the mode of interaction between hCAVII and two N, N'-disubstituted sulfamides: methyl [N-(N'benzyl)-sulfamoyl]-glycinate (sulfamide (**3**)) and methyl [N-(N'benzyl)-sulfamoyl]β-alaninate (sulfamide (**4**)), and we compared their binding modes with other structurally related inhibitors. They share the benzyl group as one of the sulfamide substituents, while the other is an aminoester derivative (glycine and β-alanine, respectively). The design of these two sulfamides was based on previous studies: other amino acid-derived sulfamides with a second aromatic substituent have shown remarkable inhibitory potency and selectivity against hCAVII [8]. Here we found out that our docking predictions about the binding mode of the two sulfamides are consistent with the classical pattern of interactions proposed between these types of inhibitors and the active site. However, these two molecules showed important differences in the proposed orientation of their substituents, probably due to the presence of an "extra" methylene group in the β-alaninate derivative (sulfamide (**4**)). Considering that our predictions have to be experimentally validated, we also report here the results of the successful synthesis of the candidates.

2   Methods

2.1   Docking Simulations

For docking simulations, we used an AutoDock4$_{ZN}$-based docking protocol previously validated both *in silico* and experimentally by us [9]. AutoDock4$_{ZN}$ is specially suitable for zinc metalloenzymes, since it extended the AutoDock4 classical force field to include a specialized function to better describe the interactions of the target with zinc-coordinating ligands.

Docking performance was previously evaluated in terms of pose prediction accuracy and virtual screening accuracy, in order to establish optimal parameters and conditions for the simulations. The pose prediction accuracy assesses the software's capacity to reproduce the experimental pose of the co-crystallized ligands within the enzyme's active site, by redocking and crossdocking simulations. The virtual screening accuracy measures the scoring function's ability to correctly discriminate between binder and non-binders using a test set of known hCAVII inhibitors and non-inhibitors (better score for active compounds). Both validation tests yielded good results, demonstrating that the docking protocol is suitable for predicting potential active candidates and their binding interactions into the hCAVII active site.

The 3D coordinates for hCAVII were taken from the Protein Data Bank (PDB-ID 3MDZ). Interestingly, this crystal structure defined two possible conformations for the side chain of one histidine residue located near the active site (HIS66) [10]. This amino acid is involved in the proton shuttle mechanism of the enzyme, which is well characterized for CAs. Based on the results of the validation protocols, we selected only one of the HIS66 conformations for the simulations: the one that orients the imidazole ring away from the active site ("out" conformation, Fig. 1), causing a bigger pocket to accommodate inhibitors into the catalytic cleft.

The docking space was set to cover the entire catalytic region of the enzyme, through a grid box of 60 x 60 x 60 Å size, considering a grid space of 0.375 Å. The 3D structures of the sulfamides (**3**) and (**4**) were generated with OpenBabel 2.4.1 at pH 7.4 and then submitted to geometry optimization with MMFF94 force field. Suitable files for docking simulations, in pdbqt format, were generated for the compounds and the target with prepare_ligand4 y prepare_receptor4 scripts, respectively. The tetrahedral zinc pseudo atom was added to the receptor with the zinc_pseudo script, and the grid parameter files (gpf) were generated with the corresponding prepare_gpf4zn script. Compounds (**3**) and (**4**) were considered as flexible, and the aforementioned out conformation of the target was kept rigid. For each sulfamide, 300 docking runs were performed, using the Lamarckian Genetic Algorithm. The population size was set to 150, the number of energy evaluations to 2500000 and the elitism to 3. All other variables were set to default values. Further details of the parameter selection criteria and validation results were described in detail in Gantner et al. [9].

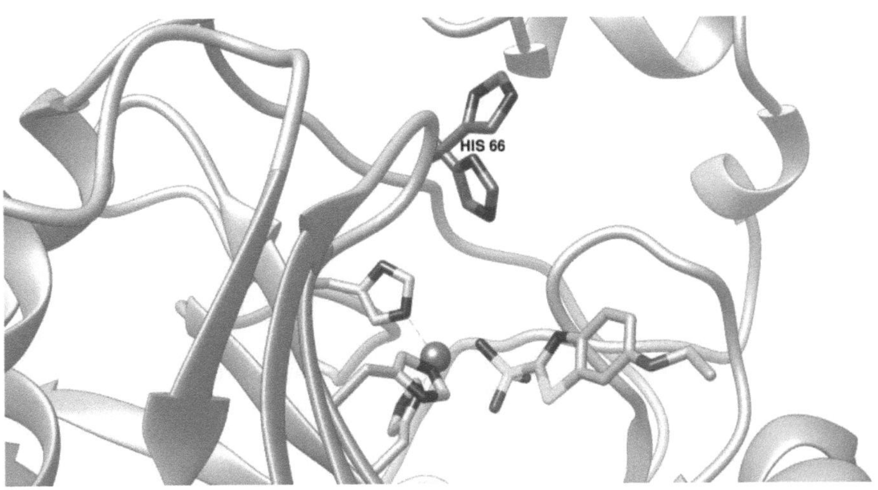

Fig. 1. hCAVII active site (PDB-ID 3MDZ) showing the binding mode of the sulfonamide ethoxzolamide (in plum). The two possible conformations of the HIS66 side chain were highlighted in medium purple sticks. The zinc ion is highlighted as a gray sphere. Hydrogen atoms were omitted for simplicity.

2.2 Chemistry

We followed one versatile synthetic route based on catechol sulfate, which allows the generation of sulfamides with different substituents (Scheme 1). It starts with the synthesis of the catechol sulfate (**1**) by the chemical reaction between catechol and sulphuryl chloride. Then, compound (**1**) reacts with benzylamine to yield a stable N-benzyl sulfamate (**2**). Finally, compound (**2**) is the reactant in common for the synthesis of the two desired products (sulfamides (**3**) and (**4**)), which proceeds after the addition of the corresponding amino esters (Scheme 1).

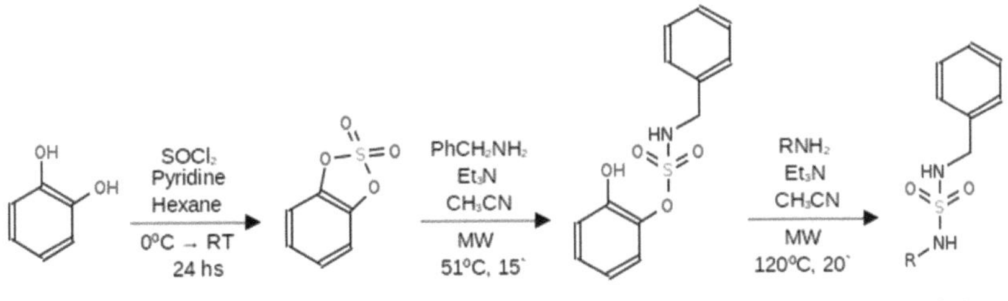

Scheme. 1. Synthetic route followed in this investigation. R = -CH$_2$-COO-CH$_3$ for compound (**3**) and R = -CH$_2$-CH$_2$-COO-CH$_3$ for compound (**4**).

Catechol sulfate (**1**) was prepared according to literature [11], using catechol and sulfuryl chloride as starting material. Regarding the synthesis of the benzyl sulfamate (**2**) and then the sulfamides (**3**) and (**4**), we followed the optimized procedures previously reported by our team for other aminoester derived sulfamides, in which we included microwave-assisted heating as an alternative to the traditional thermal heating [12]. We designed the route to first obtain the common reactant (**2**), which is used in the next step to yield the two final products. Unlike the previous investigations, benzylamine was added as hydrochloric salt (and not in its basic form), to better manipulate this reactant as a solid compound. Details about the synthesis of the compounds (**2**), (**3**) and (**4**), are reported as supplementary information.

3 Results

Table 1 summarizes the main results obtained from docking simulations. In previous investigations we defined a threshold value for the docking score (DS) during protocol validation in order to guide the selection of candidates in a virtual screening campaign [9]. This cutoff was set in -9.42, which is related with a sensitivity value around 87% and a specificity value of 75%. Compounds (**3**) and (**4**) passed this threshold, so they could be considered as potential hCAVII inhibitors in terms of the DS. It should be noted that the DS was not used as an absolute estimate of the binding free energy, but rather as a relative value that reflects the relative quality of different docking poses used for ranking and predicting binding modes.

Additionally, we calculated the theoretical ligand efficiency (LE) for the compounds. That is, the ratio between the DS and the number of heavy atoms (different from H) in the compounds. Both showed a LE above 0.5, which means that the DS is not highly dependent on the size of the candidates.

Table 1. Docking simulation results on the hCAVII for sulfamides (3) and (4).

N°	Structure	DS	LE	d	Interaction type — Hydrogen bond	Interaction type — pi stacking/ hydrophobic
(3)	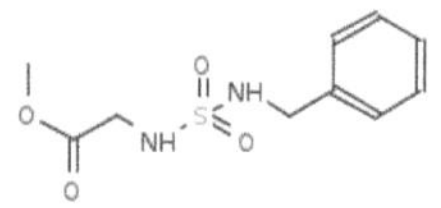	-10.29	0.61	2.1 Å	THR201 THR202	HIS96 VAL145 LEU200 VAL209 THR211
(4)	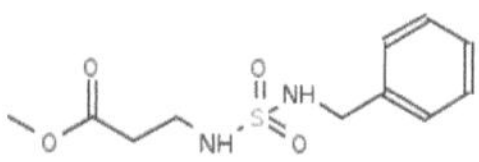	-9.71	0.54	2.3 Å	GLN94 THR201 THR202 HIS121	VAL145 VAL123 LEU143 LEU200 PHE133

DS: docking score, LE: ligand efficiency, d: predicted distance between the zinc ion and the anchoring N atom of the sulfamide.

The visual inspection of the best docking poses allowed us to propose a binding mode for compounds (**3**) and (**4**) into the hCAVII active site (Fig. 2 and Fig. 3, respectively).

As expected for classical CA inhibitors, they coordinate with the zinc ion through one deprotonated N atom, in both cases the one from the amino ester group. They also interact with the two THR characteristic residues near the zinc through hydrogen bonding interactions. Interestingly, the candidates orientate the aromatic group to different regions of the catalytic cleft. Compound (**3**) pointed the benzyl into the hydrophilic half, in order to prioritize a pi-stacking interaction with HIS96, placing the ester group closer to the catalytic center, generating a hydrogen bond with THR201 and some hydrophobic type interactions (Fig. 2). Compound (**4**) presents a longer distance between the amino and the ester group (due to an "extra" methylene group), so it can not accommodate the carboxylate into the catalytic center, and oriented it toward a less tight polar region, promoting hydrogen bonding interactions with THR202 and GLN94 residues. Then, the aromatic substituent was located in the hydrophobic region, generating numerous hydrophobic interactions with the valine, leucine, and phenylalanine residues (Fig. 3).

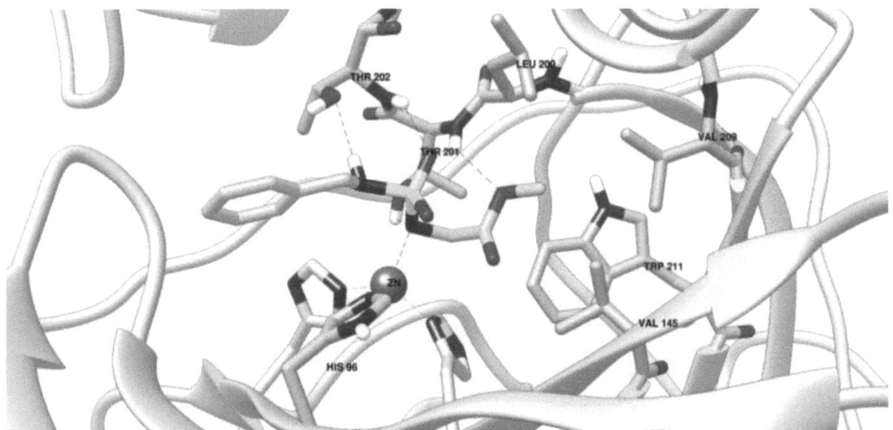

Fig. 2. Binding mode proposed by docking simulation (top score) for compound (3) (in light green sticks). Residues interacting with the ligand are shown in sky blue sticks. Some relevant interactions are shown with black dashed lines. The zinc ion is highlighted as a gray sphere. The anchoring to the zinc atom through the nitrogen atom from the amino ester group can be noted.

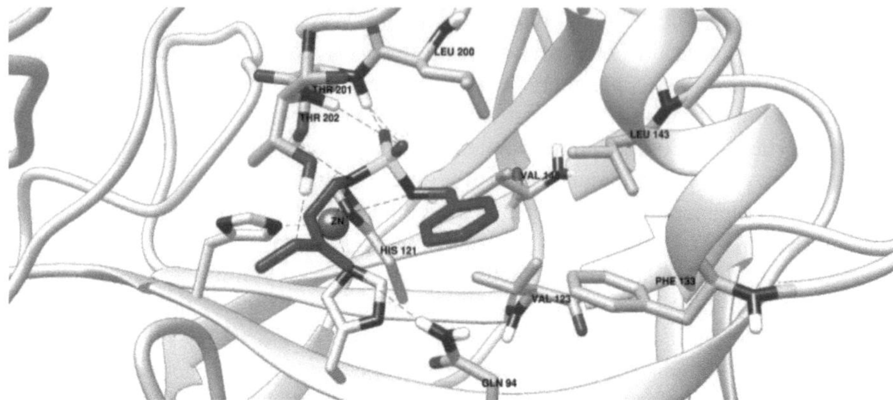

Fig. 3. Binding mode proposed by docking simulation (top score) for compound (4) (in magenta sticks). Residues interacting with the ligand are shown in sky blue sticks. Some relevant interactions are shown with black dashed lines. The zinc ion is highlighted as a gray sphere. The anchoring to the zinc atom through the nitrogen atom from the amino ester group can be noted.

As mentioned before, amino ester derived sulfamides have been previously studied as selective hCAVII inhibitors, with interesting results [8]. Among them, methyl [N-(N′-4-fluorobenzyl)]-sulfamoyl] L-valinate (compound (**5**), Fig. S1) and methyl [N-(N′-4-fluorobenzyl)]-sulfamoyl] L-phenylalaninate (compound (**6**), Fig. S2) showed the best inhibitory activity and selectivity against hCAVII. According to the docking simulations, both share the coordination with the zinc ion through the N atom of the p-fluorobenzyl group, unlike the two compounds reported here, which interacts to zinc through the N atom of the ester group. This difference could be attributed to the larger volume of the L-valinate and L-phenylalaninate substituents, acknowledging the versatility of the sulfamide function as an anchoring group. Derivatives (**5**) and (**6**) also showed the classical interactions through hydrogen bonds with the highly conserved THR201 and THR202 near the zinc. Once again, the candidates oriented the aromatic group to different regions of the catalytic cleft. Compound (**5**) was oriented in the same way as compound (**3**), with the L-valinate group on the hydrophobic side generating hydrophobic interactions, while the p-fluorobenzyl group was located on the hydrophilic side, prioritizing the formation of the pi-stacking interaction with HIS96 (Fig. S1). Conversely, compound (**6**) was oriented in the same way as compound (**4**), with the p-fluorobenzyl group on the hydrophobic side generating numerous hydrophobic interactions, while the L-phenylalaninate group was located on the hydrophilic side, promoting hydrogen bond interactions with THR202 (Fig. S2).

Regarding the synthetic procedure, Table 2 shows the main characteristics of the synthesized compounds. In case of compound (**2**), the low yield could be explained, at least in part, for the formation of the N, N′-dibenzylsulfamide as a byproduct of the reaction. That is, the desired product (compound (**2**)) could react with an additional molecule of benzylamine to yield the symmetrical N, N′-disubstituted sulfamide. In case of compound (**3**) and (**4**), the reaction involved the release of catechol as a secondary product, in equimolar quantities relative to the desired products. Therefore, the production of pure sulfamides could involve a significant loss of product in the work up process (reflected in the yield calculations). The compounds are white solids characterized by their melting point. Their identity was confirmed by the signals obtained from de ^{1}H NMR spectra.

Table 2. Relevant experimental results obtained from the synthesis of compound (2), (3) and (4).

Compound	Yield (%)	Mp (°C)	^{1}H NMR spectra (δ)
(**2**)	31	115–116	7.41–7.29 (m, 6H), 7.23–7.15 (m, 2H), 7.04 (dd, J = 8.1, 1.6 Hz, 1H), 6.91 (ddd, J = 8.2, 7.4, 1.6 Hz, 1H), 6.11 (s, 1H, -OH), 5.09 (t, J = 6.1 Hz, 1H, -NH-), 4.43 (d, J = 5.8 Hz, 2H, -CH2-)
(**3**)	15	72–72.5	7.38–7.29 (m, 5H), 4.85 (t, J = 5.7 Hz, 1H, -NH-), 4.60 (s, 1H, -NH-), 4.25 (d, J = 4.6 Hz, 2H), 3.82 (d, J = 5.4 Hz, 2H), 3.76 (s, 3H)
(**4**)	28	54–55	7.39–7.28 (m, 5H), 4.85 (t, J = 6.5 Hz, 1H), 4.51 (d, J = 6.4 Hz, 1H), 4.22 (d, J = 5.7 Hz, 2H), 3.70 (s, 3H), 3.27 (q, J = 6.1 Hz, 2H), 2.57 (t, J = 5.9 Hz, 2H)

4 Discussion

With proper diagnosis, current ASD provides seizure control in two thirds of patients [13]. Even with the existence of other alternative treatments such as surgery, the implantation of electric devices or diet therapies, there is an unsatisfied need of new drugs to fulfill the demands of pharmacoresistant patients. The exploration of new mechanisms of action could lead to the discovery of drug candidates with pharmacological profiles different from the traditional drugs. In this context, we have previously investigated hCAVII selective inhibitors, leading to compounds with remarkable anticonvulsant properties in mice. In terms of structural characteristics, the sulfamide (-NH-SO$_2$-NH-) function represents an interesting bioisosteric replacement for the classic ZBF, sulfonamide (R-SO$_2$-NH-). N, N'-disubstituted sulfamides are more versatile than sulfonamides since both nitrogen atoms are capable of acting as zinc anchors. Additionally, the disubstitution allows the possibility of accommodating two groups of diverse nature within the catalytic region of the different CA isoforms, shaping the potency and selectivity of the inhibitors.

In this investigation, we explored the binding interaction of two N, N'-disubstituted sulfamides (compound (**3**) and (**4**)) with hCAVII using a validated docking protocol. We found a pattern of interactions in the active site similar to the one proposed before for compounds of the same family. However, we proposed different orientations into the catalytic cleft for compounds (**3**) and (**4**), which can be explained by the presence of a larger distance between the sulfamide function and the ester group in compound (**4**). The promising docking score and the visual inspection of the interactions allowed us to consider both compounds as interesting candidates for hCAVII inhibition. Finally, we found that the synthesis based on catechol sulfate would be suitable for the preparation of the compound for biological testing in the near future.

Acknowledgments. This study was funded by National University of La Plata (UNLP - X1022) and Agencia Nacional de Promoción de la Investigación, el Desarrollo Tecnológico y la Innovación (PICT 2020-2077). M.E.G., L.G. and A.T. are members of Consejo Nacional de Investigaciones Científicas y Técnicas de la República Argentina (CONICET, Argentina).

Disclosure of Interests. The authors have no competing interests to declare that are relevant to the content of this article.

References

1. WHO Homepage. https://www.who.int/news-room/fact-sheets/detail/epilepsy. Accessed 25 May 2025
2. Beniczky, S., et al.: Updated classification of epileptic seizures: position paper of the International League Against Epilepsy. Epilepsia **66**, 1804–1823 (2025)
3. Hakami, T.: Neuropharmacology of antiseizure drugs. Neuropsychopharmacol. Rep. **41**(3), 336–351 (2021)
4. Gantner, M.E., Llanos, M.A., Garofalo, F.M., Villalba, M.L., Gavernet, L.: Computational and synthetic target-based approaches to the discovery of novel anticonvulsant compounds. Curr. Med. Chem. **28**(33), 6866–6894 (2021)
5. Mishra, C.B., et al.: Discovery of benzenesulfonamides with potent human carbonic anhydrase inhibitory and effective anticonvulsant action: design, synthesis, and pharmacological assessment. J. Med. Chem. **60**, 2456–2469 (2017)
6. Supuran, C.T.: Carbonic anhydrases as drug targets: general presentation. In: Supuran, C.T., Winum, Y. (eds.), Binghe B. (Series ed.), Drug Design of Zinc-Enzyme Inhibitors: Functional, Structural, and Disease Applications. 1st edn. Willey, USA (2009)
7. Gavernet, L., et al.: Inhibition pattern of sulfamide-related compounds in binding to carbonic anhydrase isoforms I, II, VII XII and XIV. Bioor. Med. Chem. **21**(6), 1410–1418 (2013)
8. Villalba, M.L., et al.: Sulfamide derivatives with selective carbonic anhydrase VII inhibitory action. Bioor. Med. Chem. **24**(4), 894–901 (2016)
9. Gantner, M.E., et al.: Identification of new carbonic anhydrase VII inhibitors by structure-based virtual screening. J. Chem. Inf. Mod. **62**(19), 4760–4770 (2022)
10. Buonanno, M., et al.: The crystal structure of a hCA VII variant provides insights into the molecular determinants responsible for its catalytic behavior. Int. J. of Mol. Sci. **19**(6), 1571 (2018)
11. DuBois, G.E., Stephenson, R.A.: Sulfonylamine-mediated sulfamation of amines. A mild, high yield synthesis of sulfamic acid salts. J. Org. Chem. **45**(26), 5371–5373 (1980)
12. Villalba, M.L., et al.: Novel sulfamides and sulfamates derived from amino esters: synthetic studies and anticonvulsant activity. Eu. J. Pharmacol. **774**, 55–63 (2016)
13. Waris, A., Siraj, M., Khan, A., Lin, J., Asim, M., Alhumaydh, F.A.: A comprehensive overview of the current status and advancements in various treatment strategies against epilepsy. ACS Pharmacol. Transl. Sci. **7**(12), 3729–3757 (2024)

Application of Machine Learning in Drug Repurposing of a New Antiseizure Drugs Active in the PTZ Kindling Model

Estefanía Peralta[1,2], Denis N. Prada Gori[1,2], Maximiliano J. Fallico[1,2], Lucas N. Alberca[1,2], Alan Talevi[1,2], and Carolina L. Bellera[1,2(✉)]

[1] Laboratorio de Investigación y Desarrollo de Bioactivos (LIDeB), Facultad de Ciencias Exactas, Universidad Nacional de La Plata (UNLP), La Plata, Buenos Aires, Argentina
`cbellera@biol.unlp.edu.ar`
[2] Consejo Nacional de Investigaciones Científicas y Técnicas (CONICET), CCT La Plata, La Plata, Buenos Aires, Argentina

Abstract. Epilepsy is a chronic neurological disorder characterized by recurrent seizures due to excessive neuronal activity. To date, there are about 30 drugs available for the treatment of epilepsy; however, approximately one-third of the patients do not achieve sustained seizure-free status with adequately chosen antiseizure medications. For this reason, the search for new therapies remains a priority. Computational tools have been extremely useful for the design and discovery of new drugs, reducing costs and time spent in the identification of novel molecular bioactive scaffolds. In this work, ligand-based computational models were developed and validated to be used in virtual screening in order to identify new drugs with promising antiseizure activity in the PTZ kindling model. Training data for the models were obtained from specialized literature, and were then representatively sampled using an *in-house* clustering procedure (iRaPCA). Linear classifiers based on conformation-independent molecular descriptors were generated using *in-house* Python routines that combine feature bagging and forward stepwise feature selection. The best classifiers obtained were combined into meta-classifiers and validated by retrospective screening experiments. Finally, the best model ensemble was applied to screen the chemical libraries DrugBank 5.1.8 and Drug Repurposing Hub (DRH), to detect potential drug repurposing opportunities for possible active drugs in the PTZ kindling model.

Keywords: VIRTUAL SCREENING · PTZ KINDLING · ANTISEIZURE · MEDICATIONS · MACHINE LEARNING

1   Introduction

Epilepsy is one of the most common neurological disorders, affecting approximately 50 million people globally across all ages, sexes and ethnicities. It is characterized by the recurrence of spontaneous seizures, leading to partial or generalized involuntary body movements due to brain damage, abnormal brain development, genetic alterations, or

© The Author(s), under exclusive license to Springer Nature Switzerland AG 2026
A. Talevi and V. Rosa Cota (Eds.): LAWCN 2025, CCIS 2734, pp. 55–66, 2026.
https://doi.org/10.1007/978-3-032-14664-9_6

brain infections, among others etiologies [1]. Because patients with epilepsy experience movements and sensory disturbances, mood disorders (such as anxiety and depression) and cognitive changes (including long- and short-term memory loss), epilepsy is a condition with a significant global burden. Consequently, it has significant economic repercussions due to health care expenses, lower work productivity of the patient and/or its relatives, and premature death [2, 3].

Currently, despite the accessibility of a wide range of antiseizure drugs, 30% of patients are unable to control their seizures via pharmacotherapy [4]. Although a wide variety of preclinical models of seizure exist for the screening of anticonvulsant drugs, in which seizures are induced in healthy animals, such as Maximal Electroshock Seizure (MES), 6 Hz and subcutaneous Pentylenetetrazol test (scPTZ) [5], these fail to represent the process of epileptogenesis or cellular and molecular alterations that occur in patients with this pathology. For this reason, the use of chronic and subchronic models has been proposed as a strategy to identify more effective therapeutic interventions [6]. Among them, kindling models generate brain damage and predisposition to seizures through successive proconvulsant stimuli, occasionally achieving a phenotype resistant to anticonvulsant drugs. One example of such models is the PTZ kindling model, where sequential chemical stimuli are administered at subconvulsive doses, generating, over time, brain changes that increase neuronal excitability and lower the seizure threshold [7].

Artificial intelligence and machine learning have proven extremely useful for various aspects of the discovery and development of new drugs, such as structure- and ligand-based virtual screening, exploration of quantitative structure-activity relationships (QSAR), drug repurposing, or toxicity and pharmacokinetic properties prediction. These technologies had a significant impact on the pharmaceutical industry, improving pharmaceutical productivity, reducing the number of unsuccessful clinical trials, and making the overall drug development cycle more time- and cost-efficient [8, 9].

QSAR models seek to establish a chemo-mathematical relationship between a chemical structure and its biological activity, allowing the identification of novel compounds with specific molecular characteristics that are fundamental to their activity [10]. The reliability of the results of QSAR models depends strongly on the quality of the information used to train the algorithm: using reliable data, selection of significant descriptors, and appropriate sampling of the training data are key to the predictivity of the models [11, 12].

Here, we have implemented computational models to search for new drug candidates to be evaluated in the PTZ kindling seizure model. For this purpose, linear classificatory QSAR models based on conformation-independent molecular descriptors were developed and then ensembled to boost their performances. The best model ensemble was applied in a prospective virtual screening campaign to explore two databases oriented to drug repositioning: DrugBank and Drug Repurposing Hub (DRH), to identify repurposed drugs with anticonvulsant activity. Noteworthy, we relied exclusively on open-source tools to implement the study.

2   Methods

Python 3.9.12 was used for the generation of the ligand-based models and for data analysis, using the scikit-learn package v1.0.2 [13], the statsmodels.api package v0.13.2 [14], the RDKit library v2022.03.3 [15], and the Plotly v4.11.0 library [16]. The steps applied in the methodology are summarized in the flowchart in Fig. 1.

2.1   Data Set Compilation and Curation

A bibliographic search was performed on Scopus and PubMed combining the keywords: "PTZ" AND "kindling" AND "mice", to identify previously reported compounds with antiseizure activity in the PZT kindling mice model.

Compounds were represented in SMILES format and standardized with the *in-house* script Listo Standardizer [17]. Duplicate molecules and compounds with inconsistent activities were excluded.

Compounds were labeled ACTIVE or INACTIVE according to the dose needed to elicit of antiseizure activity in the PTZ Kindling model: those compounds that elicited full or partial protection at doses lower or equal than 100 mg/kg were assigned to the ACTIVE class and only those compounds that elicit no protection at all were assigned to the INACTIVE class. To assess the molecular diversity of the compiled dataset, heatmaps were constructed using the *in-house* script Heatmap Similarity [17].

2.2   Dataset Splitting

The dataset was divided into three different sets: a training set, used to train QSAR linear classifier models; a validation set 1, used to validate individual QSAR models and select which models would be combined; and a validation set 2, used to evaluate the performance of the ensembled models.

To representatively sample the dataset, the *in-house* clustering algorithm iRaPCA was used with default settings [17, 18]. This clustering method is based on a combination of feature bagging, dimensionality reduction by Principal Component Analysis (PCA) and the k-means algorithm. The Silhouette coefficient was used as a validation criterion to select the optimal cluster structure that provides the best within- and between-cluster distances. Compounds from the ACTIVE and INACTIVE class were clustered separately.

2.3   Molecular Descriptor Calculation, Modelling Procedure and Model Validation

A total of 1,613 conformation-independent descriptors were computed for each compound using the molecular descriptor calculator Mordred [19]. Descriptors with a variance less than 0.05 in the training set were excluded. A combination of feature bagging and Forward Stepwise selection [20] was applied to the remaining descriptors to obtain a pool of 3,000 random subsets with 200 descriptors each. Highly correlated descriptor pairs (Pearson correlation coefficient above 0.85) within each subset were avoided and a restriction of a maximum of five descriptors per model was used to avoid overfitting. Then, a categorical dependent variable was introduced, which took a value of 1 for compounds within the ACTIVE class and 0 for compounds in the INACTIVE class. A total of 3,000 linear classifiers were obtained, one per subset, using a Forward Stepwise procedure.

The likelihood of spurious correlations and the robustness of the models were studied using Fisher randomization test and Leave-Group-Out (LGO) cross-validation, respectively. In each round of LGO, randomly stratified subsets comprising 10% of the total training set instances were held out from the training set. A total of 250 randomizations and 250 LGO folds were considered. The results of the internal validation tests were expressed as the mean accuracy across these rounds. For the LGO, results were compared with the model accuracy obtained from the original training set. In the case of Fisher randomization, the results were compared to the No Model Error Rate (NOMER) [21].

2.4 Retrospective Virtual Screening Experiments

To estimate the enrichment performance of individual and ensemble models in a real virtual screening, two retrospective virtual screening campaigns were implemented. For this purpose, known active compounds from both validation sets were seeded among a large number of putative inactive compounds (synthetic decoys), generated using our *in-house* decoy generation algorithm LUDe with default settings [22]. Enrichment metrics were calculated for the best individual and ensemble models, to assess their enrichment behavior: The Area Under the Receiver Operating Characteristic curve (AUCROC), the Boltzmann-Enhanced Discrimination of ROC (BEDROC), and the Enrichment Factor in the top-ranked 1% (EF0.01) [23, 24].

2.5 Ensemble Learning Models

The top-performing individual classifiers identified in the first retrospective screening campaign were combined into meta-classifiers, which often provide better generalization and predictivity [12, 25]. We evaluated four different combination methods: the average score (AVE), the minimum score (MIN), the average ranking (RANK) across model ensembles, and the average voting (VOT) [26].

2.6 Prospective Virtual Screening

The ensemble model that showed the best performance in the second retrospective screening campaign was used in the prospective campaign of two chemical libraries: DrugBank 5.1.8 [27] and DRH [28], both focused on chemical substances with potential for drug repurposing, e.g., approved, investigational, and withdrawn drugs.

Compounds from these databases were standardized as previously described with the *in-house* tool Listo Standardizer [17], prior to the prospective screening. The optimal cut-off value score for the ensemble model was determined by visual analysis of the Positive Predictive Value (PPV) surface [29].

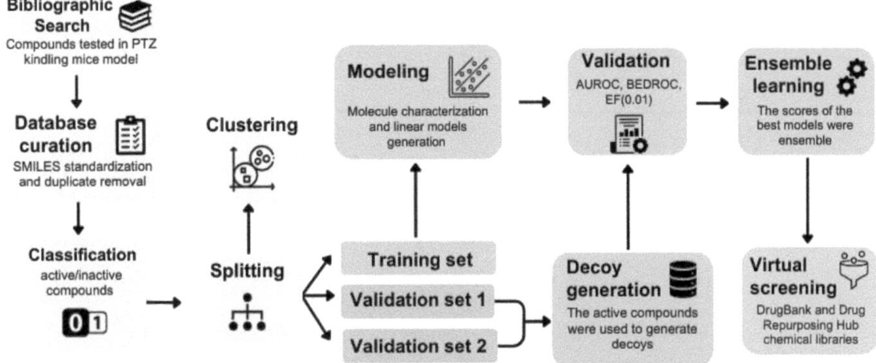

Fig. 1. Flowchart used in the present study.

3 Results and Discussion

162 compounds previously evaluated in the PTZ kindling seizure model were obtained from literature, including 81 active compounds and 81 inactive compounds (the dataset is available as Supplementary Material). The heatmap in Fig. 2 shows the molecular diversity of the compiled dataset, based on Tanimoto distances for each possible pair of compounds in the dataset. Highly dissimilar compounds contribute to intra- and inter-category structural diversity, thus indicating a relatively wide applicability domain.

iRaPCA clustering algorithm showed satisfactory performance. The active molecules were distributed into 12 clusters after four iterative rounds, obtaining Silhouette coefficients of 0.8316, 0.9023, 0.8923 and 0.8326 for the first, second, third and fourth generations of clusters, respectively. The inactive compound molecules were distributed into 9 clusters after three rounds, obtaining Silhouette values for these three iterations of 0.8784, 0.9363 and 0.6934. Cluster allocation for active and inactive compounds, with their respective SMILES, has been included in the Supporting Information as Cluster_assignation.xlsx. The active compounds from both validation sets were used as queries to retrieve synthetic decoys using LUDe. The final composition for the different data sets are presented in Table 1.

3,000 individual linear classifiers were built by applying feature bagging and Forward Stepwise on 3,000 random subsets of 200 Mordred molecular descriptors. Then, the individual models were externally validated via retrospective screening of the Validation set 1. Table 2 shows the balanced accuracy and the AUCROC for the best eight individual models according to their performance on validation set 1. The models show an acceptable active enrichment performance on validation set 1, yielding AUCROC values higher than 0.83.

The internal validation for the best eight individual models suggested that these are robust models with no spurious correlations. Results are shown in Table S1, in the Supporting Information.

An ensemble learning approach was applied to obtain meta-classifiers. Four combination approaches were considered to combine the scores of the individual models: MIN, AVE, RANK and VOT. The AVE ensemble outperformed the other combinations

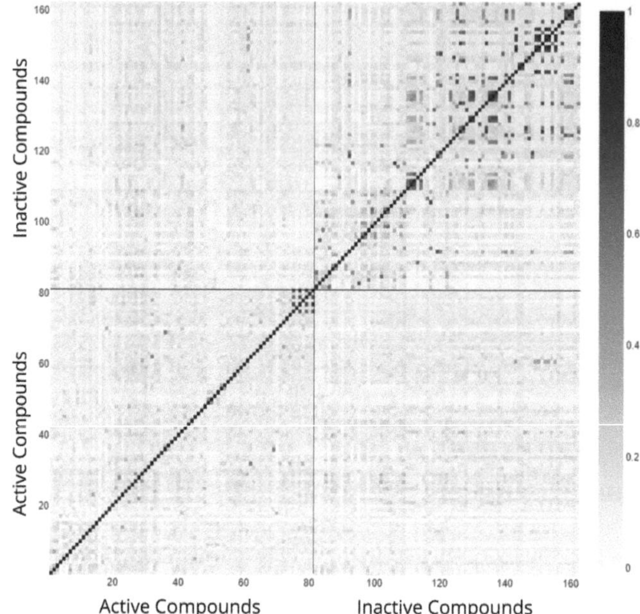

Fig. 2. Heatmap of dissimilarity for the entire database. Blue bits correspond to similar molecule pairs and pale-yellow bits correspond to dissimilar molecule pairs

Table 1. Composition of the training and validation sets.

Sets	Active compounds	Inactive compounds	Decoys
Training set	41	41	–
Validation set 1	20	20	1077
Validation set 2	20	20	820

strategies in terms of AUCROC and BEDROC. Figure 3 shows the evolution of the AUCROC and BEDROC metrics vs. the number of combined models, for the first retrospective screening campaign (validation 1) for the AVE ensemble (2- to 100-model combinations). The combination of up to eight models presented the highest BEDROC while maintaining high values of AUCROC. The enrichment metrics of this ensemble for both validation sets are presented in Table 3 and compared to Model 2206, the best individual classifier.

The score cutoff value was chosen through visual inspection of the PPV surfaces, which represent the evolution of the positive predictive value as a function of the Se/Sp ratio across a range of Ya values. The PPV surface shown in Fig. 4 was built using the data from the retrospective screening of validation set 1. Ensemble using AVE operator was applied to combine the scores of the individual models, selecting 1.080 as the score

Table 2. Balanced accuracy and AUCROC values in the training set and validation set 1 for the best eight individual models.

Individual models	Balanced accuracy		AUCROC
	Training set	Validation set 1	Validation set 1
Model 2206	0.9390	0.7431	0.8642
Model 1962	0.9024	0.7208	0.8494
Model 1953	0.9146	0.7336	0.8480
Model 667	0.9024	0.7231	0.8467
Model 2994	0.9146	0.6690	0.8406
Model 2939	0.9024	0.7200	0.8371
Model 1883	0.9024	0.7071	0.8315
Model 1146	0.9268	0.7345	0.8300

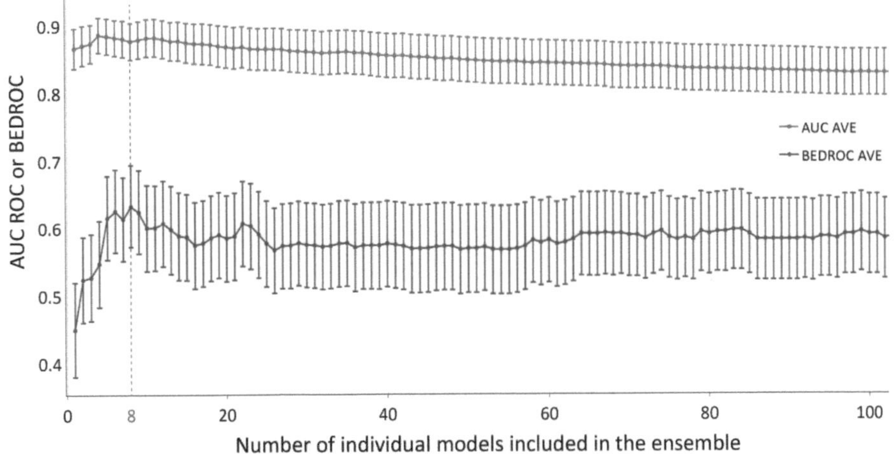

Fig. 3. AUCROC and BEDROC metrics vs. the number of combined models using the Average Score, in the retrospective screening (red points: AUCROC; blue points; BEDROC). The bars show the standard deviation (bars). The dashed line indicates the ensemble of 8 models, which was later applied in prospective virtual screening.

threshold to discriminate active from inactive compounds. This cutoff value corresponds to a Se/Sp ratio of 0.401.

Using the PPV surface, a value of 1.080 was chosen as score threshold to be used in the prospective virtual screening of DrugBank and DRH databases; such score was associated with a Se/Sp ratio of 0.401 (Se = 40% and Sp = 99%) for the 8-model ensemble based on the AVE operator, and to a PPV value $\geq$20% (PPV = 55.40) for a Ya of 0.01. This implies that, if the proportion of active molecules in the prospective

Table 3. Performance of the best individual model and the best model ensemble in retrospective screening experiments.a

Model	Validation set	AUCROC	BEDROC (alpha = 100)	EF(0.01)
Model 2206	1	0.86 ± 0.03	0.44 ± 0.07	22.59 ± 5.65
	2	0.76 ± 0.04	0.49 ± 0.08	22.68 ± 4.82
AVE-8	1	$0.88* \pm 0.03$	$0.63\dagger \pm 0.06$	$38.06\dagger \pm 4.30$
	2	$0.80\dagger \pm 0.03$	$0.53\dagger \pm 0.07$	22.69 ± 4.82

a Metric values and standard deviations for each model were obtained through bootstrapping, using 100 iterations without resampling. Metric values are statistically different from the corresponding column for the best individual model (Model 2206). * $p < 0.01$ † $p < 0.001$

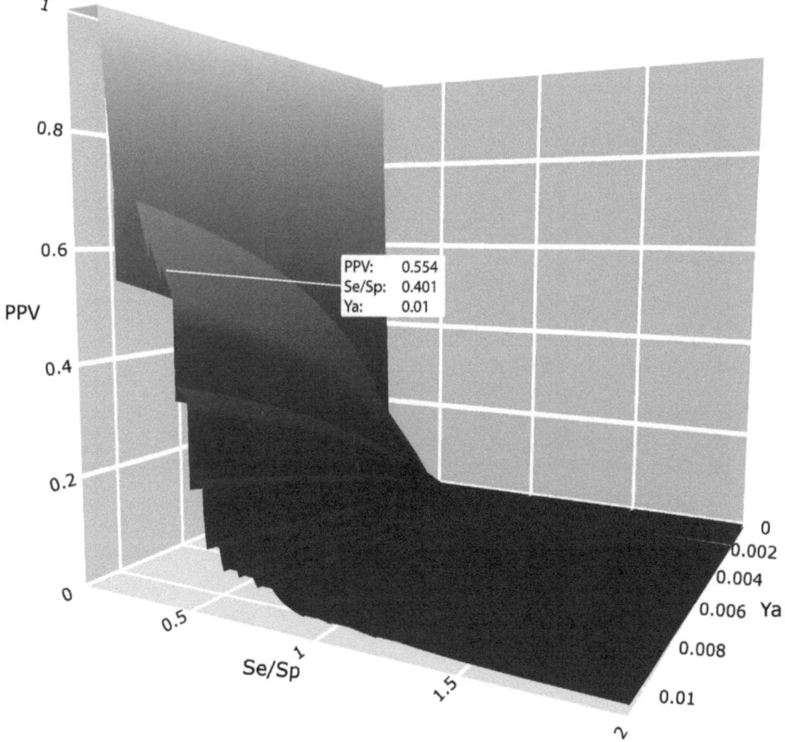

Fig. 4. PPV surface for the best ensemble on the validation set 1.

virtual screening experiment was 0.01, about five in silico hits should advance to experimental testing in order to find one confirmed hit. Considering the compounds within the applicability domain, the virtual screening of DrugBank using the previous score threshold value delivered 112 in silico hits, with 22 of them corresponding to approved drugs; in the case of the DRH database, 31 compounds surpassed the cutoff value, and 19 corresponded to approved drugs.

Table 4. Top ten in silico hits

ID	Structure	PPV(0.01)	Status	Original Use
DB02299	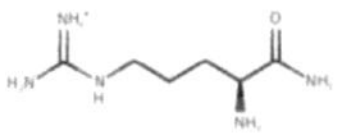	0.6598	Approved	Nutritional supplement
DB06824	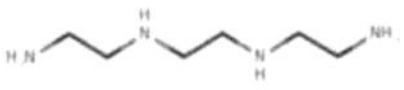	0.6598	Approved	Wilson's disease
DB05383	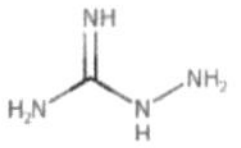	0.6598	Investigational	Diabetic nephropathy
DB00770	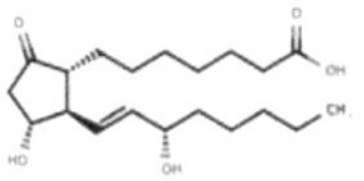	0.6598	Approved	Erectile dysfunction
DB11079	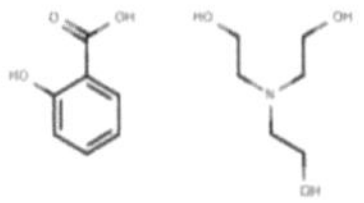	0.6598	Approved	Muscle and joint analgesic
DB15114	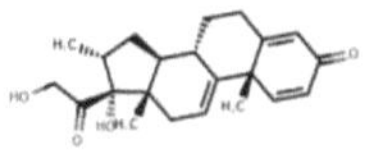	0.6244	Investigational	Duchenne muscular dystrophy
CHEMBL 3186117		0,6598	Investigational	Ointments
DB11876	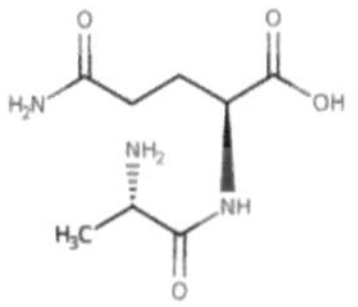	0.6244	Approved	Nutritional supplement
DB01783	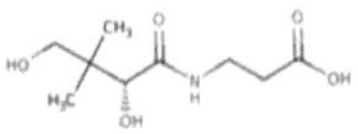	0.6244	Approved	Nutritional supplement
DB03754	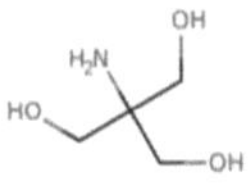	0.6244	Approved	Anti-inflammatory

The top 10 in silico hits obtained from the database screening are shown in Table 4. They include compounds with two different status: investigational drugs (compounds in clinical trials) and approved drugs. The advantage of using compounds that have passed through the preclinical phase allows for drug repositioning, an expeditive strategy for drug development that builds a new therapeutic indication based on previously collected data (e.g., pharmacokinetics, safety, and formulation data).

4   Conclusions

In this study, we applied an ensemble learning approach based on ligand-based linear classifiers. These models are capable of discriminating between active and inactive drugs in the PTZ kindling mice model, a valuable animal model to study epileptogenesis and potential antiseizure and antiepileptogenic therapies.

By combining random subspace and Forward Stepwise procedures, we obtained conformation-independent linear classifiers. Their statistical performance was subsequently improved through ensemble learning, obtaining good average and early enrichment metrics, which is noteworthy considering that our objective is to predict, based on the molecular structure, a phenotypic response in an extremely complex animal model. The cutoff score value for the best-performing model ensembles was rationally optimized through Positive Predictive Value surface analysis. This optimized cutoff value was then applied in a prospective virtual screening experiment on the DrugBank and DRH databases, resulting in 41 approved in silico hits that are direct candidates for drug repurposing.

Computer-guided drug repositioning and virtual screening using machine learning models are excellent strategies for accelerating drug development. They significantly shorten development timelines, reduce the number of experimental evaluations in animal models, and lower associated costs by leveraging existing knowledge of the pharmacological, pharmacokinetic, and toxicological, data of known drugs.

Our *in-silico* predictions will be validated experimentally in the short-term.

Acknowledgments. The authors are funded by UNLP (Incentivos UNLP and Subsidio para Jóvenes Investigadores UNLP 2024) and Agencia Nacional de Promoción Científica y Tecnológica (ANPCyT), via grants PICT 2019-00984 and PICT 2021-I-INVI-00478. L.N.A., A. T. and C.L.B. are members of the Research Career from the Argentinian National Research Council (CONICET, Argentina).

References

1. Devinsky, O., et al.: Epilepsy. Nat. Rev. Dis. Primers. **4**, 18024 (2018). https://doi.org/10.1038/nrdp.2018.24

2. Guekht, A.: Epilepsy, comorbidities and treatments. Curr. Pharm. Des. **23**(37), 5702–5726 (2017). https://doi.org/10.2174/1381612823666171009144400

3. Mula, M., Coleman, H., Wilson, S.J.: Neuropsychiatric and cognitive comorbidities in epilepsy. Continuum (Minneapolis, Minn.) **28**(2), 457–482 (2022). https://doi.org/10.1212/CON.0000000000001123

4. Dalic, L., Cook, M.J.: Managing drug-resistant epilepsy: challenges and solutions. Neuropsychiatr. Dis. Treat. **12**, 2605–2616 (2016). https://doi.org/10.2147/NDT.S84852

5. Löscher, W.: Animal models of seizures and epilepsy: past, present, and future role for the discovery of antiseizure drugs. Neurochem. Res. **42**(7), 1873–1888 (2017). https://doi.org/10.1007/s11064-017-2222-z

6. Löscher, W., Potschka, H., Sisodiya, S.M., Vezzani, A.: Drug resistance in epilepsy: clinical impact, potential mechanisms, and new innovative treatment options. Pharmacol. Rev. **72**(3), 606–638 (2020). https://doi.org/10.1124/pr.120.019539

7. Singh, T., Mishra, A., Goel, R.K.: PTZ kindling model for epileptogenesis, refractory epilepsy, and associated comorbidities: relevance and reliability. Metab. Brain Dis. **36**(7), 1573–1590 (2021). https://doi.org/10.1007/s11011-021-00823-3

8. Paul, D., Sanap, G., Shenoy, S., Kalyane, D., Kalia, K., Tekade, R.K.: Artificial intelligence in drug discovery and development. Drug Discov. Today **26**(1), 80–93 (2021). https://doi.org/10.1016/j.drudis.2020.10.010

9. Bittner, M.I., Farajnia, S.: AI in drug discovery: applications, opportunities, and challenges. Patterns **3**(6), 100529 (2022). https://doi.org/10.1016/j.patter.2022.100529

10. Gini, G.: QSAR methods. In: Benfenati, E. (eds.) In Silico Methods for Predicting Drug Toxicity. Methods in Molecular Biology, vol. **2425**. Humana Press, (New York, NY.) 1–26 (2022). https://doi.org/10.1007/978-1-0716-1960-5_1

11. De, P., Kar, S., Ambure, P., Roy, K.: Prediction reliability of QSAR models: an overview of various validation tools. Arch. Toxicol. **96**(5), 1279–1295 (2022). https://doi.org/10.1007/s00204-022-03252-y

12. Ruatta, S.M., et al.: Garbage in, garbage out: how reliable training data improved a virtual screening approach against SARS-CoV-2 MPro. Front. Pharmacol. **14**, 1193282 (2022). https://doi.org/10.3389/fphar.2023.1193282

13. Pedregosa, F., et al.: Scikit-learn: machine learning in Python. J. Mach. Learn. Res. **12**(85), 2825–2830 (2011)

14. Perktold, J., et al.: statsmodels/statsmodels: Release 0.14.0 (2023). https://doi.org/10.5281/zenodo.7899735

15. Landrum, G., et al.: RDKIT/RDKIT: 2022_03_3. Release (Release_2022_03_3) (2022). https://doi.org/10.5281/zenodo.6605135

16. Plotly Technologies Inc.: Collaborative Data Science - Plotly 2015. https://plot.ly

17. Prada Gori, D.N., Alberca, L.N., Rodriguez, S., Alice, J.I., Bellera, C.L., Talevi, A.: LIDeB tools: a Latin American resource of freely available, open-source cheminformatics apps. Artif. Intell. Life Sci. **2**, 100049 (2022). https://doi.org/10.1016/j.ailsci.2022.100049

18. Prada Gori, D.N., Llanos, M.A., Bellera, C.L., Talevi, A., Alberca, L.N.: IRaPCA and SOMoC: development and validation of web applications for new approaches for the clustering of small molecules. J. Chem. Inf. Model. **62**(12), 2987–2998 (2022). https://doi.org/10.1021/acs.jcim.2c00265

19. Moriwaki, H., Tian, Y.S., Kawashita, N., Takagi, T.: Mordred: a molecular descriptor calculator. J. Cheminf. **10**(1), 4 (2018). https://doi.org/10.1186/s13321-018-0258-y

20. El Habib Daho, M., Chikh, M.A.: Combining bootstrapping samples, random subspaces and random forests to build classifiers. J. Med. Imaging Health Inf. **5**(3), 539–544 (2015). https://doi.org/10.1166/jmihi.2015.1423

21. Gramatica, P.: On the development and validation of QSAR models. In: Reisfeld, B., Mayeno, A. (eds.) Computational Toxicology. Methods in Molecular Biology, vol. **930**. Humana Press, (Totowa, NJ.), pp. 499–526 (2013). https://doi.org/10.1007/978-1-62703-059-5_21

22. Alberca, L.N., Prada Gori, L.N., Fassio, A., Talevi, A., Bellera, C. L.: LIDEB's Useful Decoys (LUDe): a freely available decoy-generation tool. Benchmarking and scope. Artif. Intell. Life Sci. **7**, 1000129 (2025). https://doi.org/10.1016/j.ailsci.2025.100129

23. Truchon, J.F., Bayly, C.I.: Evaluating virtual screening methods: good and bad metrics for the "early recognition" problem. J. Chem. Inf. Model. **47**(2), 488–508 (2007). https://doi.org/10.1021/ci600426e

24. Saito, T., Rehmsmeier, M.: The precision-recall plot is more informative than the ROC plot when evaluating binary classifiers on imbalanced datasets. PLoS ONE **10**(3), e0118432 (2015). https://doi.org/10.1371/journal.pone.0118432

25. Hyun, J.C., Kavvas, E.S., Monk, J.M., Palsson, B.O.: Machine learning with random subspace ensembles identifies antimicrobial resistance determinants from pan-genomes of three pathogens. PLoS Comput. Biol. **16**(3), e1007608 (2020). https://doi.org/10.1371/journal.pcbi.1007608

26. Zhang, Q., Muegge, I.: Scaffold hopping through virtual screening using 2D and 3D similarity descriptors: ranking, voting, and consensus scoring. J. Med. Chem. **49**(5), 1536–1548 (2006). https://doi.org/10.1021/jm050468i

27. Wishart, D.S., et al.: DrugBank 5.0: a major update to the DrugBank database for 2018. Nucleic Acids Res. **46**(D1), D1074-D1082 (2018). https://doi.org/10.1093/nar/gkx1037

28. Corsello, S.M., et al.: The drug repurposing hub: a next-generation drug library and information resource. Nat. Med. **23**(4), 405–408 (2017). https://doi.org/10.1038/nm.4306

29. Morales, J.F., et al.: Positive predictive value surfaces as a complementary tool to assess the performance of virtual screening methods. Mini Rev. Med. Chem. **20**(14), 1447–1460 (2022). https://doi.org/10.2174/1871525718666200219130229

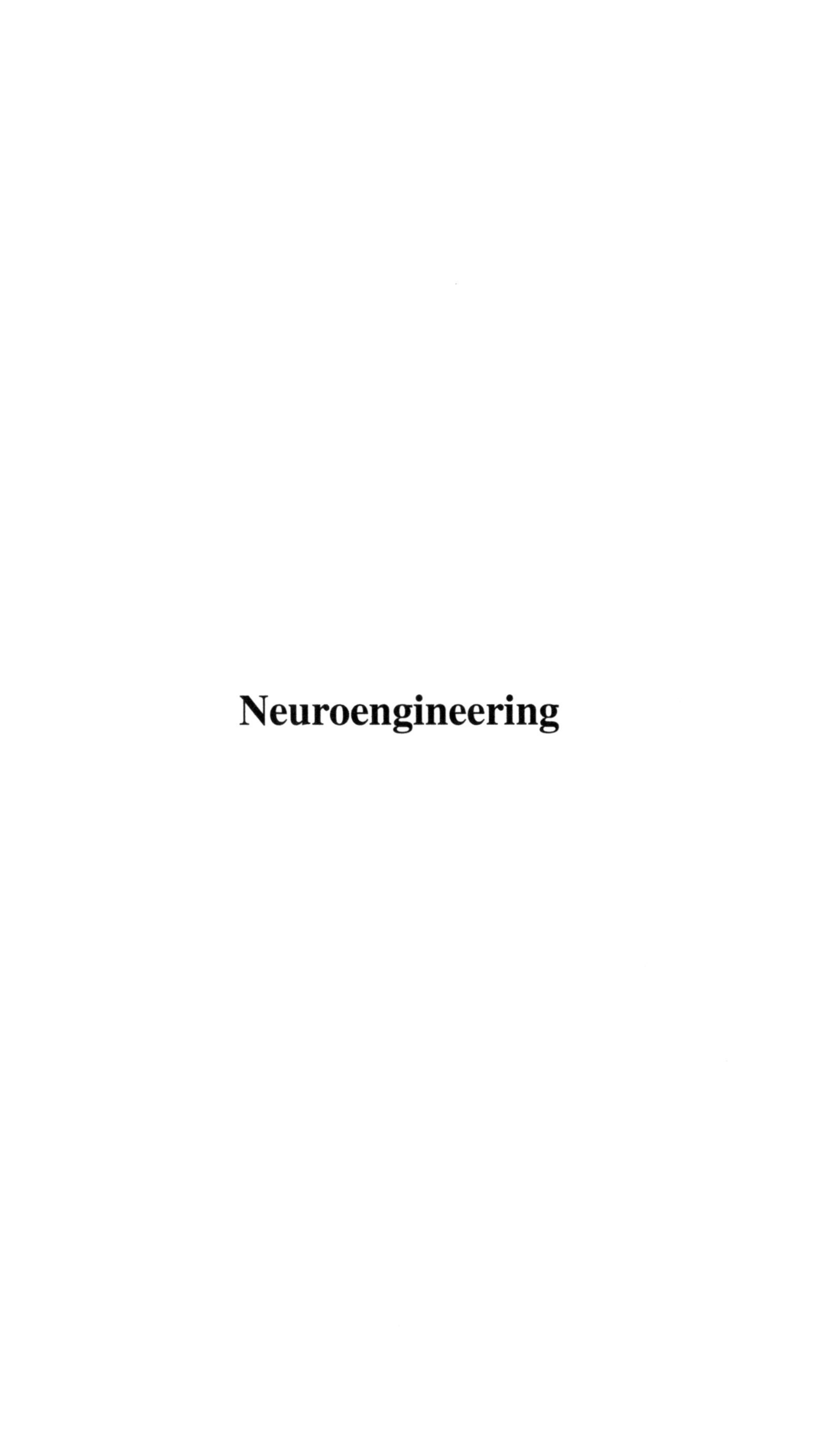

Neuroengineering

Design and Development of a Functional Prototype of an Upper-Limb Exoskeleton for Neurorehabilitation Assistance

Solana López Aguero[1,2](✉), Leandro Mayrata[1,2], Esteban Osella[1,2], and Rosa Weisz[1]

[1] Center for Rehabilitation Engineering and Neuromuscular and Sensory Research (CIRINS), Faculty of Engineering, National University of Entre Ríos (UNER), Oro Verde, Entre Ríos, Argentina
`solana.lopez@ingenieria.uner.edu.ar`
[2] Institute for Research and Development in Bioengineering and Bioinformatics (IBB), National Scientific and Technical Research Council (CONICET) – UNER, Oro Verde, Entre Ríos, Argentina

Abstract. This study presents the design, implementation, and evaluation of a low-cost upper-limb exoskeleton prototype intended to assist individuals with motor impairments, particularly those who have suffered a stroke. The device integrates a simple motorized system with 3D-printed components, emphasizing accessibility, portability, and replicability. Control loops were developed to regulate joint movements and ensure safe and effective assistance. Pilot tests conducted with healthy volunteers demonstrated the exoskeleton's potential to support upper-limb motion, although areas for improvement were identified, including comfort, ergonomics, and individual adaptability. As a future enhancement, the integration of a brushless AK60–6 V1.1 motor is proposed to improve the system's precision and dynamic responsiveness.

Keywords: Exoskeleton · neurorehabilitation · upper limb · motor control · low-cost design · home rehabilitation

1 Introduction

Population aging is a global phenomenon associated with an increased incidence of neurological and musculoskeletal disorders such as stroke, brain tumors, and degenerative diseases. These conditions frequently result in upper-limb motor impairments that reduce individuals' autonomy and quality of life. According to the World Health Organization (WHO), by 2050 one in six people in the world will be over the age of 65, with the number of people aged 80 years or older expected to triple, reaching 426 million. This demographic trend highlights the urgent need for scalable and accessible rehabilitation technologies. The WHO's Rehabilitation 2030 initiative further emphasizes the necessity of strengthening health systems and providing universal access to rehabilitation services throughout the lifespan [1].

A. Talevi and V. Rosa Cota (Eds.): LAWCN 2025, CCIS 2734, pp. 69–78, 2026.
https://doi.org/10.1007/978-3-032-14664-9_7

Robotic-assisted rehabilitation has emerged as a promising approach to address this growing demand. Several commercial devices, such as the Armeo® Spring (Hocoma), the InMotion ARM (Bionik), and the MyoPro® orthosis (Myomo), have demonstrated the potential of exoskeletons to enhance motor recovery. However, these systems are typically expensive, bulky, and limited to specialized clinical settings, making them inaccessible to many patients in low- and middle-income countries [2, 3]. Research prototypes have also explored different actuation strategies and control approaches, but many face challenges related to portability, usability, and cost-effectiveness [4–6].

From a scientific and technological perspective, significant gaps remain in the development of upper-limb exoskeletons suitable for home-based rehabilitation. The main challenges include achieving a balance between mechanical robustness and lightweight design, ensuring adaptability to different users, and enabling intuitive human–machine interaction. Moreover, most current solutions lack rigorous validation protocols to guarantee safety and reliability outside controlled laboratory environments.

Within this context, the present work introduces the design and implementation of a low-cost, 3D-printed upper-limb exoskeleton prototype developed with a user-centered approach. The system prioritizes affordability, replicability, and ease of use, aiming to bridge the gap between high-end clinical solutions and the unmet needs of patients requiring accessible home-based rehabilitation. The prototype incorporates different control modes to adapt to the user's motor condition and has been evaluated through preliminary technical tests and pilot usability studies with healthy volunteers. This paper presents the design process, the experimental validation, and future perspectives toward clinical translation.

2   Methods

We followed a user-centered design (UCD) process in three iterative phases—requirements analysis, prototyping, and evaluation—to develop a low-cost upper-limb exoskeleton for elbow flexion–extension assistance. Mechanical and electronic decisions prioritized accessibility, portability, and replicability while meeting minimum operational needs for torque and sensing sensitivity.

2.1   1Mechanical and Electronic Design

The device was built using lightweight 3D-printed parts to improve anatomical adaptability and reduce mass. As an initial step, the open-source EduExo model was employed to test motors, load cells, and control logic, providing a functional benchmark before developing the customized design. Actuation in the final prototype is provided by a DSS-M15S servomotor with integrated potentiometric position feedback, controlled by an Arduino Nano. Interaction forces were measured with a 5 kg load cell coupled to an HX711 amplifier. This architecture was selected to balance cost, local availability, and functional performance for home-rehabilitation contexts.

Key actuator specifications that guided testing include a locking torque of approximately 11.5–12 kg·cm and a stall current of 1.4–1.76 A at 6–7 V, with RC-PWM control and a 0–3.3 V feedback signal.

2.2 Control Strategies

Three modes were implemented and tested independently: (1) Position control—the joint is driven to predefined angles; (2) Impedance/assistive control—assistance scales with interaction forces measured at the forearm interface; (3) Force/resistive control—the device introduces resistive torque around a set angle. All modes used proportional feedback with empirical tuning for stable interaction.

Implementation notes and internal logs document the assistive sweep between ~ 30–120°, and a resistive "return-to-set-angle" behavior used during benchtop trials.

2.3 Validation Protocols

Validation comprised three complementary test blocks, separating acquisition procedures from analysis metrics.

1) Angular accuracy

Angular measurements from the servomotor were compared against an external digital goniometer with 0.1° resolution. Repeated elbow flexion–extension cycles were performed at 30°, 60°, and 90°, while both goniometer readings and servomotor feedback were simultaneously logged at ~ 50 Hz. Angular accuracy was quantified using Pearson correlation (r), mean absolute error (MAE), and root mean square error (RMSE). These metrics were computed by comparing goniometer and servomotor data both before and after applying the linear regression calibration described above.

2) Mechanical load and resistance

External masses ranging from 0 to 900 g were attached distally on the forearm brace, while trajectories were commanded to a 90° reference and moderate sweeps. An endurance subset was also performed with 200 consecutive cycles at ~ 60° amplitude.

The outcomes focused on trajectory deviation as a function of load and the maximum sustained load before noticeable failure or instability. Results showed minimal discrepancy at 0–100 g, increasing error beyond 500–600 g, and worst-case deviations of approximately 5.4° at 700 g. At higher loads (800–900 g), the system was unable to reliably maintain the 90° reference.

3) Safety and stability

Motor current was monitored manually during all test sessions using an inline multimeter. In parallel, actuator surface temperature was periodically measured with an infrared thermometer. No automatic current limiting or thermal shutdown was implemented; instead, operators interrupted a run whenever abnormal heating, noise, or oscillations were detected. This manual monitoring approach was consistent with previous bench observations, where oscillatory behavior emerged under restrictive/hold conditions with approximately 1 kg of resistive load.

2.4 2.4. Pilot Usability Study

A pilot study with healthy female volunteers (n = 6; 20–25 years) assessed comfort, donning/doffing, and perceived assistance. Each participant wore the device for ~ 20 min and performed simple reaching and flexion–extension under each control mode. Afterward, a structured questionnaire captured 5-point Likert ratings and open-ended comments to guide design refinements (fit/comfort across arm lengths and plastic interfaces).

3   Results

This section reports quantitative findings from laboratory validation and pilot testing. Results are presented according to the predefined validation protocols.

3.1   Final Design

The exoskeleton prototype was manufactured using 3D-printed PLA parts and assembled with the selected electronics. The CAD model is shown in Fig. 1, while Fig. 2 presents the functional prototype worn by a healthy volunteer. The device demonstrated an anatomically adaptable and lightweight configuration, suitable for preliminary usability testing.

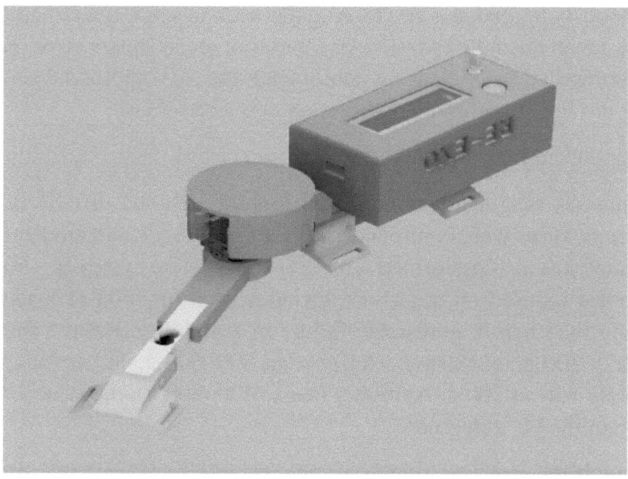

Fig. 1. 3D CAD model of the final prototype.

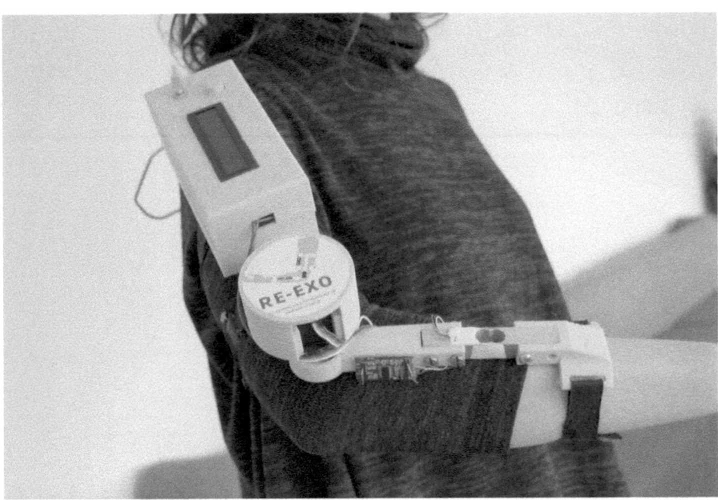

Fig. 2. Final prototype of the RE-EXO upper-limb exoskeleton during pilot testing with a healthy volunteer.

3.2 Angular Measurement Accuracy

Comparison between goniometer and servomotor feedback revealed a systematic deviation that increased with joint amplitude. After linear regression calibration, the mean absolute difference was 4.72°, equivalent to 10.49% of the mean reference value across trials.

As shown in Fig. 3, servomotor readings consistently overestimated goniometer measurements, with deviations most pronounced at larger amplitudes. The quantitative results are summarized in Table 1, which reports mean goniometer and servo values, absolute errors, and correlation coefficients for the three tested amplitudes.

Table 1. Comparison between goniometer and servomotor readings during flexion–extension cycles.

Target Angle	Mean Goniometer (°)	Mean Servo Feedback (°)	Error (°)	Pearson r
30°	29.8	30.5	0.7	0.97
60°	59.5	61.2	1.7	0.95
90°	89.8	95.0	5.2	0.91

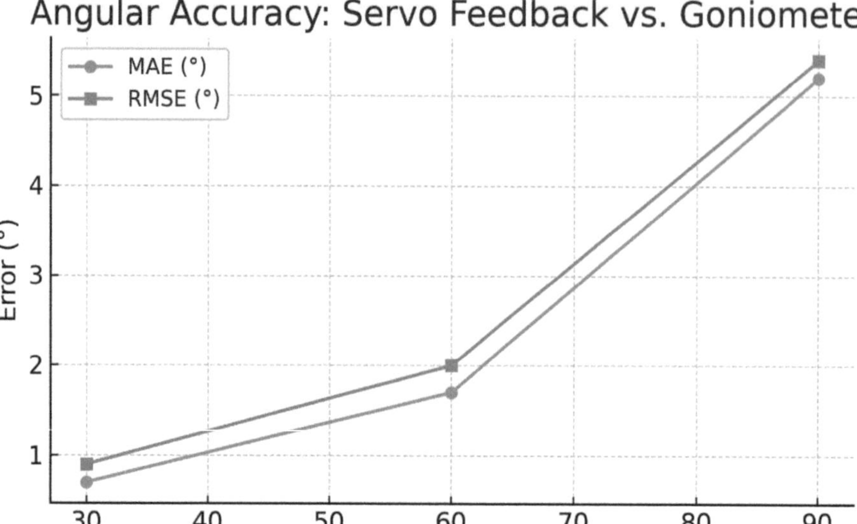

Fig. 3. Comparison between goniometer and servomotor feedback during flexion–extension cycles.

3.3 Load and Mechanical Resistance Tests

Angular precision decreased as external loads increased. For light loads (0–100 g), discrepancies remained minimal ($\pm 0.2°$). Beyond 500 g, errors increased significantly, reaching a worst case of $5.4°$ at 700 g. At > 800 g, the system could not maintain the $90°$ reference reliably.

This behavior is illustrated in Fig. 4, which shows the progressive loss of accuracy under increasing external loads.

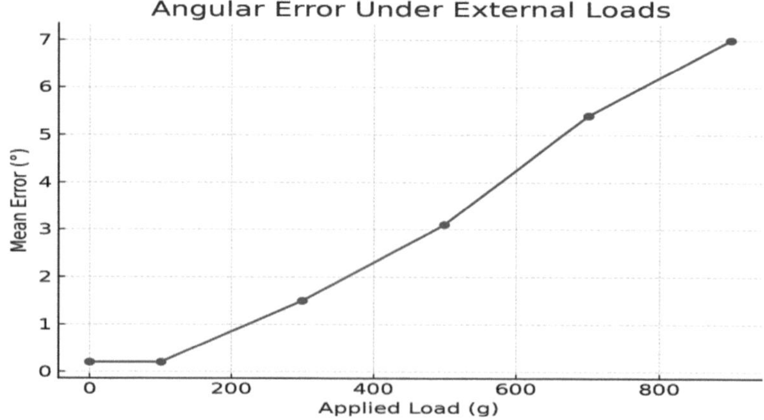

Fig. 4. Angular error under increasing external loads.

3.4 Safety and Stability Observations

No automatic current or temperature limits were implemented. Monitoring was performed manually using an inline current sensor and an infrared thermometer. No unsafe conditions were observed during short test sessions, although oscillations appeared in resistive/hold mode with ~ 1 kg load. This highlights the need for integrated safety features in future iterations.

3.5 Pilot Usability Tests

Six healthy female volunteers (20–25 years old) participated. Each wore the device for ~ 20 min under all three control modes.

Quantitative ratings are summarized in Fig. 5.

- Comfort: 3.7 ± 0.5
- Donning/doffing ease: 4.2 ± 0.4
- Perceived assistance: 4.0 ± 0.6

Participants described the prototype as *lightweight* and *easy to use*, while also suggesting softer interfaces at the forearm and better adjustability for different arm lengths.

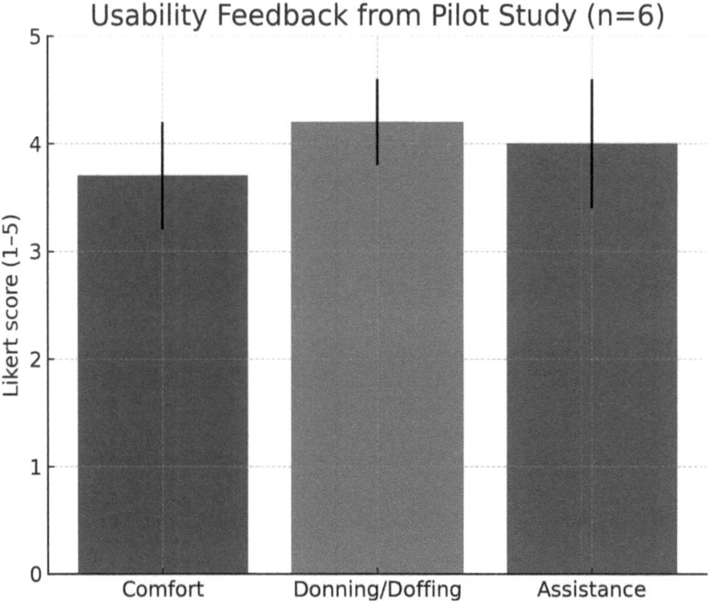

Fig. 5. Usability feedback from six healthy volunteers (Likert scale ratings).

4 Discussion

The present work focused on the development of a low-cost, home-oriented upper-limb exoskeleton for elbow flexion–extension assistance. The prototype was conceived as an accessible and replicable solution, aiming to bridge the gap between expensive commercial systems and the need for affordable rehabilitation tools in resource-limited contexts.

4.1 Mechanical and Electronic Design Considerations

Preliminary tests were conducted using the open-source EduExo platform, which provided a baseline for evaluating motor performance, load-cell integration, and control logic. Building upon this foundation, the final prototype introduced a 3D-printed PLA structure that reduced weight and enabled anatomical customization, differentiating it from bulkier commercial solutions such as Armeo® Spring or InMotion ARM. The use of accessible components (Arduino Nano, DSS-M15S servomotor, HX711 amplifier) allowed for rapid prototyping and validation, though these choices imposed limitations on long-term robustness and clinical applicability.

A key finding was the narrow margin between actuator capability and biomechanical requirements. The DSS-M15S exhibited a nominal torque of 1.57 Nm, only slightly above the estimated requirement of ~ 1.4 Nm. This estimation was obtained from anthropometric data: for an average adult forearm and hand ($\approx$2.3–2.5 kg) with a center of mass located ~ 0.16 m from the elbow joint, the static torque is ~ 1.4 Nm. This value is consistent with torque demands reported in upper-limb biomechanics literature [9, 10]. While sufficient for preliminary testing, this limited margin became evident under higher loads, where angular precision deteriorated and oscillations emerged.

4.2 Evaluation and Testing Considerations

The systematic deviation observed between servomotor feedback and goniometric measurements emphasizes the need for higher-resolution sensors and more robust calibration. Angular accuracy was acceptable under light loads but degraded significantly beyond 500–600 g, confirming the torque limitation. The absence of integrated safety features—such as automatic current limiting or thermal shutdown—was mitigated by manual monitoring during laboratory tests, but future iterations must include embedded protections to ensure safe, unsupervised use.

Pilot usability tests with healthy volunteers confirmed the potential of the design, reporting overall effectiveness and ease of use, but also underscored areas requiring improvement: comfort, forearm interface design, and adaptability across different anthropometries. These insights reinforce the importance of incorporating user feedback early in development cycles.

4.3 Comparison with Related Work

Compared with commercial systems like Armeo® Spring (Hocoma), InMotion ARM (Bionik), and MyoPro® (Myomo), the present prototype prioritizes affordability and replicability over advanced sensing or actuation. While these devices provide clinically validated control strategies, their high cost and clinical-only deployment limit accessibility, particularly in low- and middle-income settings. The proposed exoskeleton contributes by demonstrating that functional assistance can be achieved with low-cost components, though at the expense of precision and robustness.

Similar research prototypes reported in the literature often explore advanced control strategies (e.g., EMG-driven or adaptive assist-as-needed), yet few address the challenge of scalability for home use. Our findings highlight that even with simplified control loops, usability and portability can be achieved, provided that future iterations incorporate stronger actuators, more reliable sensing, and integrated safety.

4.4 Future Directions

Based on the lessons learned, the next generation of the prototype will integrate a high-performance brushless motor (CubeMars AK60–6 V1.1), which supports position, current, and velocity control via CAN communication, and provides real-time feedback (temperature, voltage, current, error codes). This upgrade is expected to overcome the torque limitations observed with the DSS-M15S, while enabling safer and more adaptive strategies.

Further development should also include:

- Improved ergonomic interfaces (padding, adjustable straps).
- Embedded safety layers (hardware current limiting, thermal shutdown).
- Validation with patient populations under standardized rehabilitation tasks.

5 Conclusion

This work presented the design and preliminary validation of a low-cost, 3D-printed upper-limb exoskeleton prototype intended for home-based rehabilitation. Built upon the EduExo platform and refined through iterative design, the prototype demonstrated the feasibility of achieving functional elbow flexion–extension assistance with accessible components. Laboratory validation confirmed systematic deviations in angular accuracy and load-dependent performance limitations, primarily due to the narrow torque margin of the selected actuator.

Pilot usability tests with healthy volunteers highlighted the system's potential for portability and ease of use, while also revealing the need for improved comfort, adaptability, and integrated safety features. Compared with commercial systems, the prototype contributes by emphasizing affordability and replicability, addressing accessibility challenges in low- and middle-income contexts.

Future work will focus on upgrading actuation with a CubeMars AK60–6 brushless motor, integrating embedded safety mechanisms, and extending validation to patient populations under standardized rehabilitation protocols. These steps will be essential to transform the prototype into a robust, clinically applicable system for home rehabilitation.

References

1. World Health Organization. *Rehabilitation 2030 Initiative.* Available: https://www.who.int/initiatives/rehabilitation-2030
2. Hocoma. *Armeo® Spring.* Available: https://www.hocoma.com/us/solutions/armeo-spring-2/

3. Bionik. *InMotion ARM*. Available: https://scholarworks.utrgv.edu/cgi/viewcontent.cgi?article=1078&context=som9331

4. Myomo. *MyoPro®*. Available: https://myomo.com/

5. Han, P.-P., et al.: Enriched environment-induced neuroplasticity in ischemic stroke and its underlying mechanisms. Front. Cell. Neurosci. (2023)

6. Singh, N., et al.: Evidence of neuroplasticity with robotic hand exoskeleton for post-stroke rehabilitation: a randomized controlled trial. J. NeuroEng. Rehabil. (2021)

7. Braun, R. G., Wittenberg, G. F.: Motor recovery: how rehabilitation techniques and technologies can enhance recovery and neuroplasticity. *Semin. Neurol.* (2021)

8. Posteraro, F., et al.: Robot-mediated therapy for paretic upper limb of chronic patients following neurological injury. J Rehabil Med **41**(12), 976–980 (2009)

9. Bhujel, S., Hasan, S.: A comparative study of end-effector and exoskeleton type rehabilitation robots in human upper extremity rehabilitation. *Human-Intell. Syst. Integr.* (2023)

10. Langhorne, P., et al.: Stroke rehabilitation. Lancet **377**(9778), 1693–1702 (2011)

11. van Kordelaar, J., et al.: Impact of time on quality of motor control of the paretic upper limb after stroke. Arch. Phys. Med. Rehabil. **95**(2), 338–344 (2014)

12. Waddell, K.J., et al.: Feasibility of high-repetition, task-specific training for individuals with upper-extremity paresis. Am. J. Occup. Ther. **68**(1), 1–10 (2014)

13. Lang, C.E., et al.: Dose response of task-specific upper limb training in people at least 6 months poststroke. Ann. Neurol. **80**(3), 342–354 (2016)

14. McCabe, J., et al.: Comparison of robotics, functional electrical stimulation, and motor learning methods for treatment of persistent upper extremity dysfunction after stroke. Arch. Phys. Med. Rehabil. **96**(5), 981–990 (2015)

15. Iwamoto, Y., et al.: Does frequent use of an exoskeletal upper limb robot improve motor function in stroke patients? Disabil. Rehabil. **44**(11), 2231–2238 (2022)

16. Martínez-García, A.B., et al.: Mechanical properties of 3D-printed parts made of polyethylene terephthalate glycol. J. Mater. Eng. Perform. **30**(10), 7356–7367 (2021)

An Inverted Perspective for the Reference Electrode and a Heuristic Metric for Spectra-Temporal Mapping of EEG Signals Aiming at Motor-Imagery Classification

Gabriel Chaves de Melo[1]([⊠]), Sheher Bano Zaigham[2], Bruna Mezzari Carlos[1],
Pedro Felipe Giarusso de Vazquez[1], Cassio V. Ruas[1], and Gabriela Castellano[1]

[1] Gleb Wataghin Institute of Physics, UNICAMP, Campinas SP 13083-859, Brazil
`chaves1135@gmail.com, gabriela@unicamp.br`
[2] Department of Ocean System Engineering, Jeju National University, Jeju 63243,
Republic of Korea

Abstract. Electroencephalography (EEG) is the most commonly used brain imaging technique for Brain-Computer Interfaces (BCI). Despite its advantages (e.g., safety, cost, time resolution), the intra-subject signal variability poses a major challenge for robustness and accuracy of BCI systems. Two main causes of this variability are the low spatial resolution and the active reference electrode, both responsible for including components from non-task-related cortical areas in the recorded data. In this work, we propose an inverted perspective towards the reference electrode, which relies on looking at a multichannel monopolar set as a collection of information from the reference. Moreover, we propose a heuristic metric that accounts for signal variability and class separability to quantify the potential of each channel to be used for classification between two motor imagery (MI) tasks. The strategy was tested in two datasets and the results reveal strong dependency on the frequency, rather than the scalp region, with the best results occurring for the delta band. Also, the interval which contains the best features for classification depends more on the delay after the MI instruction (~3 to 4 s) than on the activity being performed.

Keywords: Electroencephalography (EEG) · Reference Electrode · Signal Variability

1 Introduction

Electroencephalography (EEG) is the most used brain imaging technique for Brain-Computer Interfaces (BCI) [1]. Its popularity is due to practical and safety reasons, since it has a time resolution in the order of milliseconds, it is portable and cost-affordable, besides being non-invasive and not offering any risks for the users [2]. EEG allows detection of motor imagery (MI) activity, which is essential for BCIs. MI is the mental simulation of movement without actual physical execution. It results in modulation of sensorimotor rhythms, particularly in the mu (8–13 Hz) and beta (13–30 Hz) frequency bands [3]. BCI remains mainly in the scientific research domain, rarely being used in practical scenarios [4, 5]. The main reason for this is the limited accuracy BCI systems still present in identifying correct mental states in real-time [6]. The major challenge that limits the accuracy is the EEG signal variability, both inter- and intra-subject, which has been reported since the early days of the BCI field [7].

EEG's low spatial resolution, caused by the volume conduction between the cortex and the scalp that mixes signals from different cortical areas before they reach the electrodes [8], is one of the reasons for the variability. Alongside spatial resolution, the active reference problem stands as a major obstacle, given that any scalp region is active in terms of cortical activity, causing the reference electrode to be active as well, regardless of its location [9, 10]. Therefore, any EEG channel will include cortical activities from the two electrodes forming the channel, the so-called main and reference electrodes, in such a way that all recordings should be considered as bipolar (between two active sites) instead of as monopolar (one active site referenced to a null site) [8, 11].

Typically, bipolar recordings in the EEG field are assessed by channels with closely spaced electrodes and are commonly used in clinical scenarios [8]. Monopolar recordings are usually multichannel, with all the main electrodes referenced to a single reference. In the context of single trial or real-time analysis (which is the case for BCI applications), the approach towards the reference can be to choose a specific reference supposedly with minimum activity compared to the other electrodes or to apply a transformation to the signals to eliminate or attenuate the reference contribution to the recordings. In the first case, the choice is often linked to the EEG signature of interest but commonly varies among linked mastoids or electrodes at the 'z' line (sagittal plane) [11]. However, this is more common in offline analyses, because trial-averaging can reduce the reference contribution, and it is not possible to know in advance if a certain location has in fact a reduced contribution to the recordings or not [11, 12]. In the second case, which is commonly adopted in BCI scenario, there are three well-known transformations: common average reference (CAR) [13], reference electrode standardization technique (REST) [14], and surface Laplacian (SL) [15, 16]. After applying the desired transformation, the recordings from all the available electrodes are treated as true signals from the corresponding underneath region of the cortex. Both CAR and REST are mathematical solutions to the reference problem as stated in the work of Yao and colleagues [17] with consistent physical meaning. They are formulated to eliminate or at least attenuate the reference contribution to the recordings. SL has a solid physical and mathematical background as well and mathematically eliminates the reference contribution by transforming the original voltage signals into the variation of current density along the direction orthogonal to the scalp. However, all three approaches share limitations due to mathematical uncertainties, unrealistic assumptions of head geometry, unprecise knowledge of electrical properties of the volume conductor, and limited number of electrodes. These limitations have been extensively described and demonstrated throughout literature [18–23]. So far, no definite solution for the reference problem has been accepted by consensus in the literature [12].

In this work, we tackle the reference issue by inverting the typical perspective of a monopolar EEG set. Instead of considering the reference as null or something to be eliminated, we propose an approach that sees the monopolar set as a collection of information about, precisely, the reference site. This is the exact opposite of the common practice throughout literature. However, it originates from a direct and undeniable observation: the one cortical activity that is unquestionably present in all monopolar channels is that which is detected by the reference electrode. Thus, this novel approach opens a new route to assess the reference electrode issue. Here, we use two publicly available motor-imagery (MI) EEG datasets to re-reference the original signals to all the electrodes, one-at-time, to extract the most information about the reference site and generate a new signal. Then, after transforming all the original signals, we propose a heuristic metric that combines intra-subject reproducibility (or its inverse, variability) and class separability to discriminate between two motor imagery classes. This metric is used to provide a score for each electrode site in consecutive 1 s intervals of the task, for different frequencies, so we can analyze the best channels over time and separate by frequency bands. This allows us to find the best EEG signatures for classification purposes in a BCI and to propose more robust strategies for the signal processing pipeline.

2   Methods

Two EEG datasets with left- and right-hand motor imagery signals were used. The datasets are referred to here as GNF in reference to the group that made it available – *Grupo de Neuro-Física*, in Portuguese – (16 electrodes, 15 subjects, stroke patients) [24] and LEE in reference to the first author of the article with this dataset (62 electrodes, 15 subjects, healthy subjects) [25]. In both cases, multiple trials took place consecutively alternating randomly between left- and right-hand MI tasks.

For signal processing, all the procedures were executed with Matlab R2021a. Signals were first segmented into epochs, according to their experimental procedure, and separated by their MI. The epochs segmentation for both datasets is shown in Fig. 1.

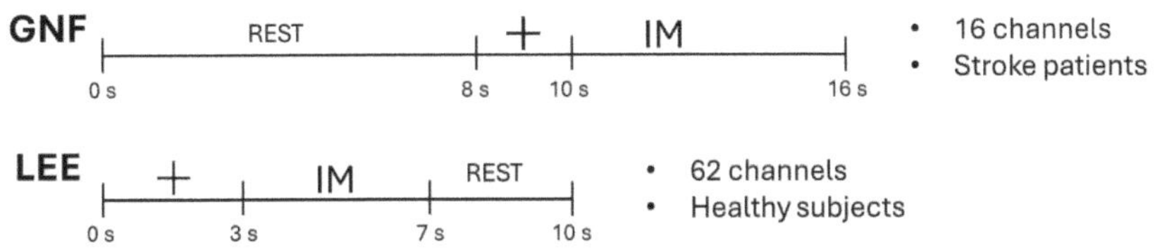

Fig. 1. Epoch segmentation according to the experimental paradigm of each dataset.

The EEG signals were transformed according to the following procedure: a) an electrode was selected, and the EEG original data were re-referenced to this electrode; b) the principal component analysis (PCA) algorithm was applied to set the first principal component as the new signal for the specific location of the reference electrode; c) the procedure was repeated for all electrodes, providing a new set of transformed EEG data.

A metric to provide scores for each channel was proposed (Eq. 1), the reproducibility and separability score (RASS). The metric aims to find scalp sites and trial's sub-intervals that would likely contain signals related to the task and with information to distinguish between left- and right-hand MIs. To perform this analysis, trials were divided into 1 - second intervals and these intervals were analyzed separately. The main assumption to evaluate how much a signal was directly related to the task was that task-related signals should have low inter-trial variability, which is the same as high inter-trial reproducibility.

The inter-trial variability was measured by the average magnitude squared coherence (MSC, or simply Coh) between multiple pairs of 1 s segmented signals from different trials of the same MI and corresponding to the same 1 s interval within the trial. Higher Coh values indicate lower variability. We called this the reproducibility score (RS), and it was calculated separately for each MI and each sub-interval of the trial. Coh was calculated for frequencies between 1 Hz and 32 Hz. To measure how much the signal would probably be effective for MI separability, Coh was calculated across pairs of corresponding intervals from each MI. Coh values vary between 0 and 1. In this case, lower Coh values indicate higher separability between classes. We called this the separability score (SS). See Fig. 2 for a schematic representation. The frequency range from 1 to 32 Hz was divided into eight sub-bands for both the RS and SS: 1–4 Hz (delta), 4–8 Hz (theta), 8–12 Hz (alpha), 12–16 Hz (beta 1), 16–20 Hz (beta 2), 20–24 Hz (beta 3), 24–28 Hz (beta 4), 28–32 Hz (beta 5). Finally, the heuristic measure RASS was proposed by combining inter-trial variability RS and MI discriminability SS for each channel, frequency band, and task sub-interval, as shown in Eq. 1.

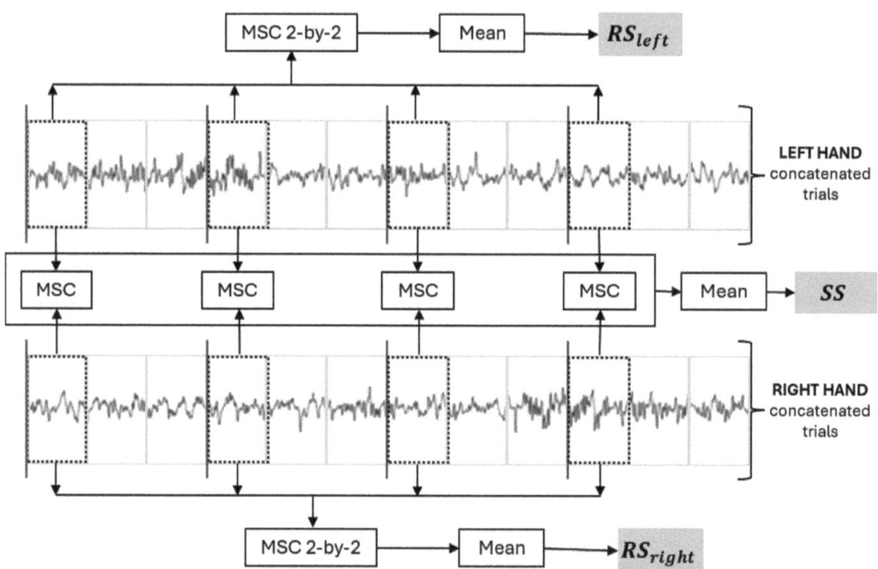

Fig. 2. Calculation of the RS and SS parameters using MSC for the first hypothetical interval of the task, delimited by black-pointed rectangles. Red vertical lines indicate the beginning of each repetition (trial); the light-gray rectangular divisions indicate the different intervals for which the parameters were calculated. Upper and lower signals correspond to concatenated repetitions of the task in which the same MI occurred (left or right hand).

$$RASS = \frac{RS_{left} + RS_{right}}{10^{SS}} \tag{1}$$

In the denominator, SS is the power of 10 to attenuate its impact on RASS. Because SS values are typically low, if they were used alone in the denominator, they would have a much greater impact on RASS than RS values. For instance, $SS = 0.1$ and $SS = 0.3$, both low values, would equalize the RASS value for two hypothetical cases for RS values such as $RS_{left} = RS_{right} = 0.2$ and $RS_{left} = RS_{right} = 0.6$, respectively, both resulting in a RASS of 4. On the other hand, with the proposed equation the values would be 0.32 ($SS = 0.1$; $RS_{left} = RS_{right} = 0.2$) and 0.60 ($SS = 0.3$; $RS_{left} = RS_{right} = 0.6$). With the proposed metric, the score range of RASS lies between 0 and 2.

3   Results

Figures 3 and 4 show the RASS represented as a heat map for each interval and cortical region for the datasets GNF and LEE, respectively. Each plot corresponds to a different subject. For GNF, intervals 1 and 2 correspond to the rest phase (3 s and 4 s length, respectively), interval 3 corresponds to the cross on the screen (2 s length), and intervals 4 and 5 correspond to the MI cue on the screen (3 s length each). For LEE, interval 1 corresponds to the cross on the screen (3 s length), intervals 2 and 3 correspond to the MI cue on the screen (2 s length each), and intervals 4 and 5 correspond to the rest phase (1 s and 2 s length, respectively).

The electrodes were grouped into six regions: F-L, F-R, C-L, C-R, P-L, P-R, representing left and right hemispheres of frontal, central and parietal regions, respectively. In Figs. 3 and 4, the color bars indicate the subject's minimum, median and maximum. On the horizontal axis, time intervals are represented. Within each interval there are eight values aligned horizontally for each scalp region; they correspond to each frequency band in ascending order, and they can only be viewed by the color changes in the figure, because they are not explicitly indicated in the horizontal axis. Therefore, the horizontal axis represents simultaneously the time intervals and the frequency bands for each time interval. This totals 240 values on each plot (5 intervals x 8 frequency bands x 6 scalp regions). These 240 values are plotted as a continuous smooth surface for better visualization of general patterns.

The first thing that draws attention is the pattern of vertical columns for all subjects. This suggests a high dependence on the frequency band rather than on the scalp regions. A closer look shows that all intervals begin with high values and finish with low values, which is an inverse relation with the frequency: lower frequencies are associated with higher RASS values.

In general, it is not clear that there is any pattern concerning the intervals, although individually it can be observed for a few subjects. A few examples are: GNF – S2 shows increasing values for the intervals, GNF – S3 shows the same, although a little less pronounced, GNF – S5 has higher values for interval 4, LEE – S1–4–5–6–9–12 have higher values for interval 4 (note that intervals for GNF and LEE do not correspond necessarily to the same trial events).

Another interesting observation is that, in general, the median value for each subject is very close to the minimum value compared to the maximum.

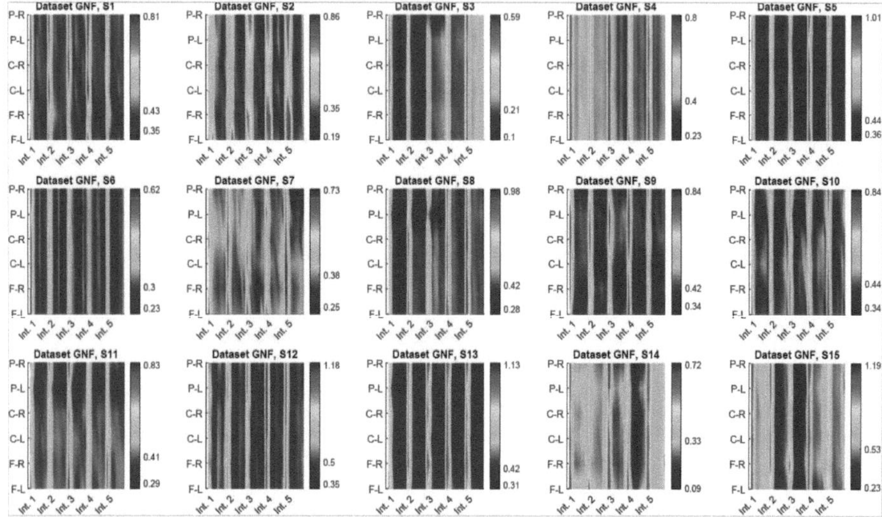

Fig. 3. Individual RASS for each subject from dataset GNF. The vertical axis is the scalp region, horizontal axis is the task interval, further divided into the eight frequency bands (see Methods), and the color represents the score (RASS), with color range varying between subject's minimum and maximum. Next to each graphic, the color bar indicates the maximum, median, and minimum values. The results are discrete values (one value per scalp region, per interval, per frequency band), but they were smoothly interpolated for better visualization.

Figures 5 and 6 show the boxplots for RASS according to the frequency band, interval, and scalp region. In each case, the RASS were averaged across all the other variables, including subjects. These figures are based on values from Figs. 3 and 4 but organized differently to highlight different features.

In Fig. 5, the pattern concerning the frequency band previously mentioned is now explicit. For both datasets, the delta band stands out, followed by the theta band. For the GNF dataset, the boxes are distributed across a higher range, approximately 0.2 to 1.0, while for LEE the boxes are distributed between approximately 0.5 to 0.9.

In Fig. 6, the average RASS for each interval across all subjects is presented. For clarity purposes, we shall designate the two rest intervals as R-1 and R-2, the MI intervals as M-1 and M-2, and the cross interval as C. The intervals in Fig. 6 were reordered so corresponding intervals from both datasets became aligned, starting with C, which refers to the cross interval.

For the GNF dataset the highest value is for interval 5, which is the second half of the MI performance. Interval 1, which is immediately after interval 5 (because the trials are performed repeatedly most of the time) also has a high value, very close to that of the first half of the MI. The lowest value is for the interval with the cross on the screen (interval 3).

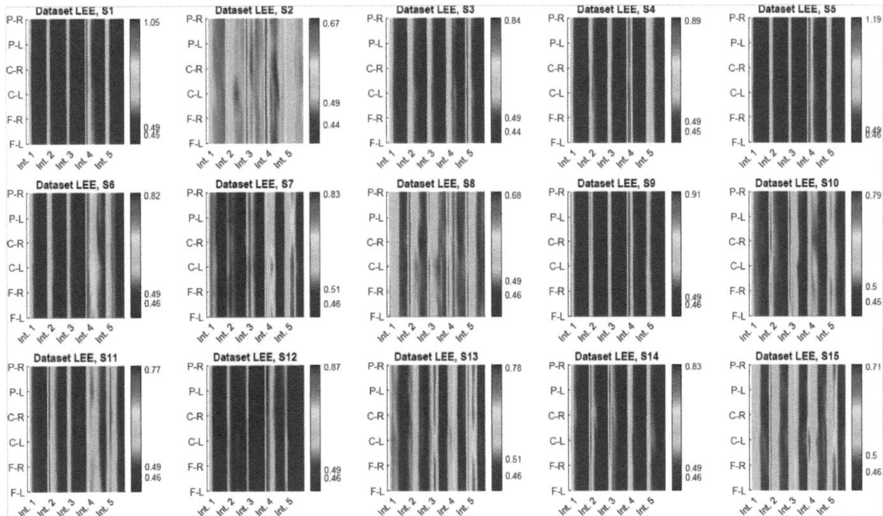

Fig. 4. Individual RASS for each subject from dataset LEE. The description is the same as for Fig. 3.

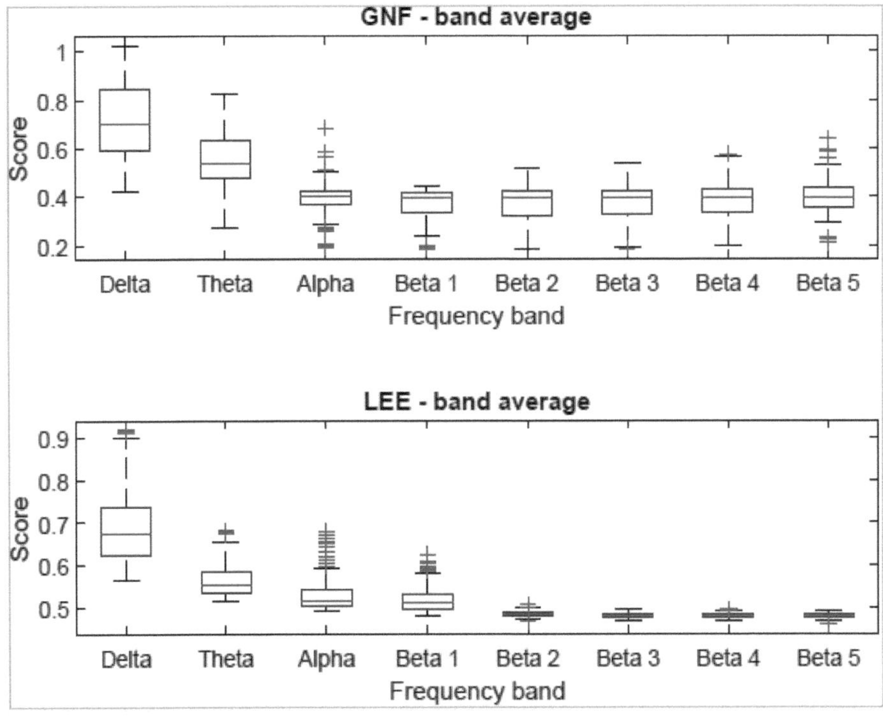

Fig. 5. Boxplot with the average RASS across all subjects from dataset GNF (upper graphich) and dataset LEE (lower graphic) for each frequency band, regardless the task interval and scalp region.

For the LEE dataset the highest value occurred for interval 4, immediately after the MI performance, followed by interval 5, which remains in the resting phase post MI. The lowest value is for interval 1, which corresponds to the cross on the screen, just like for GNF.

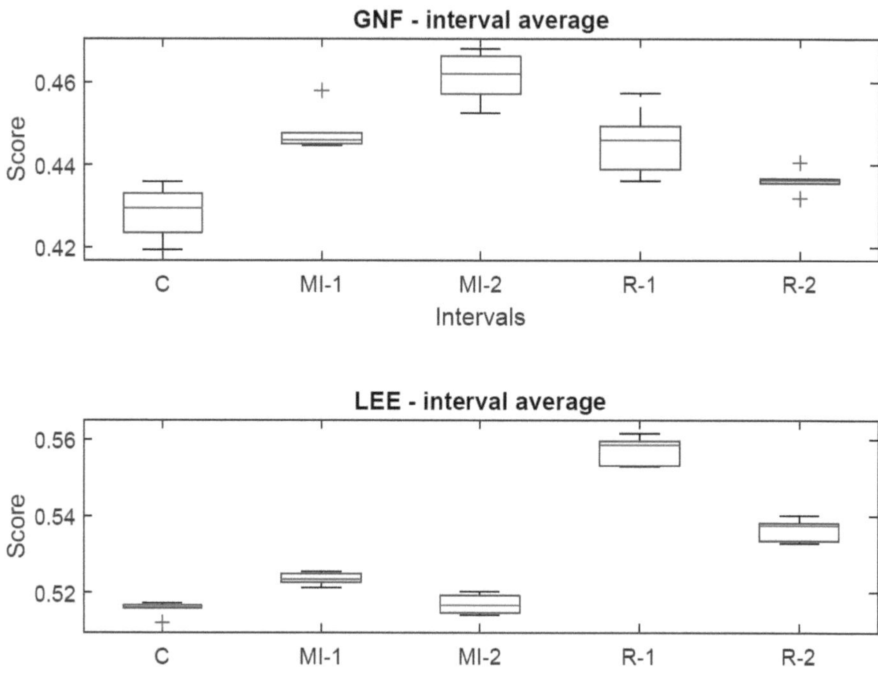

Fig. 6. Boxplot with the average RASS across all subjects from dataset GNF (upper graphich) and dataset LEE (lower graphic) for each task interval regardless the frequency band and scalp region. In the horizontal axis, C refers to the cross interval, MI-1 and MI-2 refer to two consecutive intervals with the MI cue on the screen, R-1 and R-2 refer to two consecutive rest intervals in between trials.

4 Discussion

In this work, a transformation is proposed for the signals to reduce the active reference effect combined with a metric, RASS, to score channels, task sub-intervals and frequency bands according to the signal's capacity to provide reproducible and class-discriminable MI signals. The strategy was applied to two datasets, one of which contains data from healthy subjects and the other with data from stroke patients. The similarity in the results from both datasets suggests that the strategy was effective and indicates some level of robustness, especially because the conditions of the participants differ from one another.

An interesting finding from the results refers to the intervals that showed the highest RASS values. In Fig. 6, the best results in descending order were: MI-2, R-1, MI-1, R-2, C for GNF; and R-1, R-2, MI-1, MI-2, C for LEE. The only matches between GNF and

LEE in this case were MI-1 and C, in the 3rd and 5th positions, respectively. The best RASS in each case is intriguing, M-2 for GNF and R-1 for LEE, especially for the LEE dataset, because it is neither of the intervals with motor-imagery. However, the lengths of the intervals are different for both datasets, due to their different total length (see Fig. 1). By analyzing the intervals in terms of seconds and synchronizing them with $t = 0$ s at the end of interval C (which coincides with the MI cue appearance), we found that the results for both datasets shared major similarities. For instance, the highest scores were in intervals ranging from 3 to 6 s (GNF) and 4 to 5 s (LEE), followed by 6 to 9 s (GNF) and 5 to 7 s (LEE), then 0 to 3 s (GNF) and 0 to 2 s (LEE), then, in 4th position, 9 to 13 s (GNF) and 2 to 4 s (LEE), and finally in the last position for both datasets, the C interval. Therefore, it can be stated that the interval which contains the best features for classifying between left- and right-hand MIs according to the proposed metric depends on the delay after the cue appearance (~3 to 4 s), regardless of the ongoing activity, whether the task is being performed or has already finished. This has a major impact on the development of classification algorithms, because it goes against the common practice that considers solely the interval in which the MI is being performed. Most times this interval is almost entirely inside the first 3 seconds [6, 26, 27] and the algorithms still struggle to provide accurate and robust performances.

Another notable finding concerns the delta band being the most determinant aspect to generate the best signals in terms of reproducibility and separability (Figs. 3, 4 and 5). This agrees with the results from de Melo and colleagues [12] in which a different dataset was used, a different metric was applied to measure the reproducibility, and delta band results were significantly better than other bands. Also, slow potentials included in the delta band have been shown to be effective for classification of motor tasks [28]. However, the alpha and beta bands, both known to be related to motor activity [29] and commonly the first choices for analyzing motor task signals [11, 30] did not show good results.

These two findings suggest that EEG late-slow potentials, currently under-explored, might be key for MI discrimination in BCIs. This hypothesis encourages further investigation, especially by means of mapping the RASS along with their complete scenario specification, i.e., task interval, channel (or scalp region), and frequency band. The assessment of the time-features of signals with highest RASS and the evaluation of the RS and SS scores separately are encouraged as well.

Finally, in Figs. 3 and 4 the distribution of the individual RASS within each plot draws attention, because for all subjects, half of the values are concentrated very close to the minimum score, while the other half is usually in a much higher range. This reinforces the need for strategies to search among multiple variables to find good signals for classification purposes. Moreover, the variation of maximum values across subjects shows that subjects perform differently in terms of EEG motor imagery signals, despite the clear patterns observed across all subjects and datasets.

Overall, results show that the inverted perspective for the reference electrode provides consistent information throughout subjects and conditions (healthy subjects and stroke patients). This encourages future research to explore different strategies other than PCA to extract information from a monopolar dataset to attribute it to the reference electrode. Moreover, the RASS approach with separate scores for reproducibility – which accounts for general task-related features – and for separability – which accounts for MI-specific features – can be explored in future research to perform a refined evaluation of the signals and their band-scalp distribution in terms of these two parameters. Vazquez and colleagues [31] also proposed separate scores for reproducibility and separability. In their work, they analyzed functional connectivity parameters to extract statistical measures of class distribution (average and standard deviation) and quantify both scores. Our heuristic metric, on the other hand, considers the comparison of single-trial signals directly, which allows a better link between the scores and the signals themselves with their spectra-temporal and spatial features.

Acknowledgement. This research was supported by São Paulo Research Foundation – Brazil (FAPESP) – Grants #2013/07559–3, #2015/03695–5, #2020/16571–0, #2022/08057–0, #2023/11024–0, #2025/10963–8, and #2023/12422–9, Brazilian National Council for Scientific and Technological Development (CNPq) – Grant #304008/2021–4, and Brazilian Studies and Projects Funding (FINEP) - Grant 2140/22.

References

1. Peksa, J., Mamchur, D.: State-of-the-art on brain-computer interface technology. Sensors (Basel) **23** (2023)
2. Lebedev, M.A., Nicolelis, M.A.L.: Brain-machine interfaces: from basic science to neuro-prostheses and neurorehabilitation. Physiol. Rev. **97**, 767–837 (2017)
3. Pfurtscheller, G., Neuper, C.: Motor imagery and direct brain-computer communication. Proc. IEEE **89**, 1123–1134 (2001)
4. Guo, Z., Gao, Q., Jiang, Y., Jiang, H., Jiang, N.: Therapeutic effects of brain-computer interface on motor recovery of stroke patients: a meta-analysis. medRxiv, 1–30 (2023)
5. Elashmawi, W. H., et al.: A comprehensive review on brain–computer interface (BCI)-based machine and deep learning algorithms for stroke rehabilitation. Appl. Sci. (Switzerland), vol. 14 Preprint at https://doi.org/10.3390/app14146347 (2024)
6. Guerrero-Mendez, C.D., et al.: Enhancing complex upper-limb motor imagery discrimination through an incremental training strategy. Biomed. Signal Process. Control **99**, 106837 (2025)
7. Vidal, J.J.: Toward direct brain-computer communication. Annu. Rev. Biophys. Bioeng. **2**, 157–180 (1973)
8. Wolpaw, J. R. & Wolpaw, E. W. Brain-Computer Interfaces: Principles and Practice. (2012)
9. Geselowitz, D. B.: The zero of potential. IEEE Eng. Med. Biol. Magaz. **17** (1998)
10. Nunez, P.L., Srinivasan, R.: Electric Fields of the Brain: The Neurophysics of EEG. Oxford University Press, Oxford (2006)
11. de Melo, G.C., Castellano, G., Forner-Cordero, A.: Identification and analysis of reference-independent movement event-related desynchronization. Biomed Phys Eng Express **11**, 025001 (2025)
12. de Melo, G.C., Castellano, G., Forner-Cordero, A.: A procedure to minimize EEG variability for BCI applications. Biomed. Signal Process. Control **89**, 105745 (2024)
13. Bertrand, O., Perrin, F., Pernier, J.: A theoretical justification of the average reference in topographic evoked potential studies. Electroencephalogr. Clin. Neurophysiol., 462–464 (1985)
14. Yao, D.: A method to standardize a reference of scalp EEG recordings to a point at infinity. Physiol. Meas. **22**, 693–711 (2001)

15. Hjorth, B.: An on-line transformation of EEG scalp potentials into orthogonal source derivations. Electroencephalogr. Clin. Neurophysiol. **39**, 526–530 (1975)
16. Perrin, F., Pernier, J., Bertrand, O., Echallier, J.F.: Spherical splines for scalp potential and current density mapping. Electroencephalogr. Clin. Neurophysiol. **72**, 184–187 (1989)
17. Yao, D., et al.: Which reference should we use for EEG and ERP practice? Brain Topography, vol. 32, pp. 530–549 Preprint at https://doi.org/10.1007/s10548-019-00707-x (2019)
18. Junghöfer, M., Elbert, T., Tucker, D.M., Braun, C.: The polar average reference effect: a bias in estimating the head surface integral in EEG recording. Clin. Neurophysiol. **110**, 1149–1155 (1999)
19. Qin, Y., Xu, P., Yao, D.: A comparative study of different references for EEG default mode network : the use of the infinity reference. Clin. Neurophysiol. **121**, 1981–1991 (2010)
20. Liu, Q., et al.: Estimating a neutral reference for electroencephalographic recordings: the importance of using a high-density montage and a realistic head model. J Neural Eng **12** (2015)
21. Chella, F., Pizzella, V., Zappasodi, F.: Impact of the reference choice on scalp EEG connectivity estimation. J. Neural Eng. **13**, 1–21 (2016)
22. Hu, S., Lai, Y., Valdes-sosa, P.A., Bringas-vega, M.L., Yao, D.: How do reference montage and electrodes setup affect the measured scalp EEG potentials? J. Neural Eng. (2018). https://doi.org/10.1088/1741-2552/aaa13f
23. Srinivasan, R., Nunez, P.L., Tucker, D.M., Silberstein, R.B., Cadusch, P.J.: Spatial sampling and filtering of EEG with spline laplacians to estimate cortical potentials. Brain Topogr. **8**, 355–366 (1996)
24. Carlos, B. M. *et al.* Graph network and symmetry analysis after combined XR and tDCS in stroke rehabilitation. Biomed. Signal Process Control **96** (2024)
25. Lee, M. H., et al.: EEG dataset and OpenBMI toolbox for three BCI paradigms: An investigation into BCI illiteracy. Gigasci. **8** (2019)
26. Özkahraman, A., Ölmez, T., Dokur, Z.: Determination of the common electrodes for users and increasing the classification accuracy of motor imagery EEG. Neural Comput. Appl. **37**, 5057–5076 (2025)
27. Miao, Y., et al.: Learning common time-frequency-spatial patterns for motor imagery classification. IEEE Trans. Neural Syst. Rehabil. Eng. **29**, 699–707 (2021)
28. Ofner, P., Schwarz, A., Pereira, J., Müller-Putz, G.R.: Upper limb movements can be decoded from the time-domain of low-frequency EEG. PLoS ONE **12**, 1–24 (2017)
29. Pfurtscheller, G., Lopes, F.H.: Event-related EEG/MEG synchronization and desynchronization: basic principles. Clin. Neurophysiol. **110**, 1842–1857 (1999)
30. Zapała, D., et al.: Motor imagery perspective and brain oscillations characteristics: Differences between right- and left-handers. Brain Res Bull **220** (2025)
31. Vazquez, P. F. G., de, Stefano Filho, C. A., Melo, G. C., de, Forner-Cordero, A., Castellano, G.: Reproducibility analysis of functional connectivity measures for application in motor imagery BCIs. Biomed Signal Process Control **85** (2023)

Beyond Full Electrode Arrays: Optimizing Channel Selection for Motor Imagery BCIs via Individual Channel Classifiers and Ensembles

Jaime A. Riascos-Salas[1,2]($\boxtimes$) , Hernán Villota[2] , and Marta Molinas[3]

[1] Potsdam University, Potsdam, Germany
`riascossal@uni-potsdam.de`
[2] Institución Universitaria de Envigado, Envigado, Colombia
[3] Norwegian University of Science and Technology, Trondheim, Norway

Abstract. Motor Imagery Brain-Computer Interfaces (MI-BCIs) based on Electroencephalography (EEG) enable endogenous communication using the mental rehearsal of motor actions without performing real movements. Core challenges faced by MI-BCI include user discomfort from electrode caps, signal variability across individuals and recording sessions, and the high dimensionality and noisiness of EEG data, which complicates feature extraction and classification. Current literature primarily focuses on global channel reduction or feature selection strategies to overcome the high-dimension EEG problem. This study introduces a novel methodology to improve MI-BCIs classification rates by training individual classifiers for each EEG channel, diverging from traditional full-array electrode approaches. We evaluated this method in offline training and pseudo-online settings (simulating real-time EEG signal using unseen data), comparing its performance, both for individual channel classifiers and ensembles (Stacking, Majority Vote), against established feature extraction and selection techniques: Filter Bank Common Spatial Patterns (FBCSP), and Minimum Redundancy Maximum Relevance (mRMR). Our approach uses power bands (Theta, Alpha, Beta, Gamma) to train several classifiers (SVM, MLP, KNN, and LDA). Initial evaluation of the full set of 256 individual channel classifiers revealed suboptimal performance, often below mRMR and FBCSP. However, selecting the top-10 individual channel classifiers per subject significantly boosted accuracy by approximately 20%, with all subjects outperforming FBCSP and several surpassing mRMR. This highlights the potential of localized, personalized channel subsets over uniform electrode coverage. In over-time classification, the Stacking ensemble achieved consistent high accuracy, even when individual classifiers showed high variability. This framework offers a computationally efficient and personalized solution for MI-BCI, particularly promising for real-time adaptive systems.

Keywords: Channel Reduction · FBCSP · mRMR · Ensemble · Brain-Computer Interface · Motor Imagery

© The Author(s), under exclusive license to Springer Nature Switzerland AG 2026
A. Talevi and V. Rosa Cota (Eds.): LAWCN 2025, CCIS 2734, pp. 90–108, 2026.
https://doi.org/10.1007/978-3-032-14664-9_9

1   Introduction

Motor Imagery Brain-Computer Interfaces (MI-BCIs) represent a well-established paradigm for endogenous, active communication with external devices [23]. Successful MI-BCI applications span control of wheelchairs [24], videogames [3], virtual reality environments [15], and prostheses [22]. These interfaces leverage the mental rehearsal of motor limb movements without physical execution, eliciting characteristic Event-Related Synchronization (ERS) and Desynchronization (ERD) in the mu and beta bands within the sensorimotor cortex, primarily at C3, Cz, and C4 electrode sites [13]. These sensorimotor rhythms (SMRs) are extensively studied and widely exploited in BCI research [11,25].

MI-BCI systems fundamentally rely on the acquisition and processing of electroencephalography (EEG) signals to decode SMRs into actionable output commands. However, the practical deployment of EEG-based BCIs faces several inherent challenges. Users often experience discomfort and fatigue from wearing electrode caps for prolonged periods, and head or body movements can introduce significant artifacts into the EEG signal [4]. Furthermore, achieving robust and consistent classification performance is complicated by the substantial variability of EEG signals both across individuals and between recording sessions [21].

Within the BCI pipeline [14], feature extraction and classification constitute the core components. This critical stage demands careful consideration of neurophysiological phenomena specific to the user's task, often requiring manual (or deep learning-driven automatic) definition of discriminative features and their underlying brain regions [14]. EEG data, frequently collected from a large number of channels (exceeding 100 in some high-density setups), present inherent noisiness, redundancy, and high dimensionality. These characteristics escalate computational complexity, prolong setup times, and increase the risk of overfitting classification models, ultimately diminishing BCI efficiency and usability [18]. Consequently, identifying and selecting an optimal, minimal subset of EEG channels is vital for reducing computational load, enhancing classification accuracy, and improving overall system performance. The challenge of reliably selecting EEG channels for MI-BCI has driven substantial research since 2010, leading to a diverse array of techniques often adapted from feature selection algorithms, source representation, and filtering principles [1]. Prominent channel and feature selection methods include:

Common Spatial Pattern (CSP): CSP is a widely adopted spatial filtering technique for MI-EEG analysis, designed to maximize variance differences between (or across) motor imagery classes. Filter Bank Common Spatial Pattern (FBCSP), a notable variant, applies CSP to EEG signals decomposed into multiple frequency bands via a bank of band-pass filters [2]. FBCSP has demonstrated particular utility in improving MI-BCI classification accuracy [9,20], especially when combined with dynamic visual stimuli. For instance, Lin and Chen [9] reported that FBCSP-LDA achieved an average accuracy of 73.23% with a low false positive rate (23.76%) in a dynamic MI experiment. While FBCSP can reduce computational complexity compared to a single broadband approach, it may still necessitate a large electrode array and extended operational times.

Minimum Redundancy Maximum Relevance (mRMR) Feature Selection: mRMR is a prominent filter-based feature selection method that identifies an optimal subset of features maximizing relevance to the classification task while minimizing redundancy among themselves [12]. In MI-BCI, mRMR selects discriminative features from various domains, including spatial (e.g., CSP-derived), temporal, and spectral features across multiple frequency sub-bands. Javidan et al. [7] demonstrated mRMR's effectiveness, achieving an average accuracy of 79.1% using approximately 42.4 features on the BCI 2008–2b dataset, underscoring its capability in selecting dominant features for MI-BCI classification.

Genetic Algorithm (GA) Optimization for Source Estimation: Recent work has also explored automated methodologies for optimal selection of minimum electrode subsets, particularly for accurate EEG source estimation. For instance, Soler et al. [19] proposed an optimization-based study using the Non-dominated Sorting Genetic Algorithm II (NSGA-II) to concurrently minimize localization error and the number of required EEG electrodes. This method demonstrated that optimal subsets with as few as 6 electrodes can achieve equal or better accuracy than high-density EEG (HD-EEG) with over 200 channels for a single source case in both synthetic and real signals, and 8-channel combinations for multiple sources. This approach emphasizes selecting electrodes based on their contribution to estimation accuracy rather than uniform scalp coverage, highlighting that not any subset of channels can achieve such accuracy, but rather optimized combinations for a particular brain source configuration.

The existing literature primarily focuses on global channel reduction or feature selection strategies to optimize overall classification accuracy by identifying a single optimal subset of channels applicable across all trials or subjects. However, the inherent complexity and variability of the human brain mean that optimal channels for MI tasks can differ significantly across individuals, brain areas, and even within sessions. This paper introduces a novel approach: training individual classifiers for each EEG channel and subsequently leveraging ensembles of these single-channel classifiers. This departs from the conventional paradigm by investigating whether localizing the classification effort to individual channels, and then combining their outputs, can offer a more personalized, computationally efficient, and robust solution for MI-BCI, particularly for real-time applications.

2   Materials and Methods

Our experimental design follows a typical Brain-Computer Interface (BCI) pipeline, encompassing data acquisition, preprocessing, feature extraction, classification, and feedback. This study specifically focuses on refining the feature extraction and classification stages [14].

2.1 EEG Motor Movement/Imagery Dataset Physionet

We utilized the publicly available EEG Motor Movement/Imagery Dataset from PhysioNet [16]. This dataset comprises electroencephalography (EEG) data from 109 participants performing and imagining various movements. Recordings were acquired using the BCI2000 system at a sampling rate of 160 Hz, with 64 electrodes positioned according to the international 10–10 system. For this initial investigation, we randomly selected data from 10 participants (subject IDs: 20, 22, 24, 37, 44, 51, 71, 82, 93, 98).

Out of 14 runs per subject (including baseline and 12 task-specific runs equally divided between motor imagery and motor execution), our experiment focused on runs 4 and 8 for training. These runs specifically involved imagined left and right fist movements. Run 12, also containing imagined left or right fist movements, was reserved as an unseen test set for over-time classification. Each two-minute task run file contained 15 Motor Imagery (MI) or Motor Execution (ME) trials, each lasting four seconds and preceded by a relaxation period [17].

2.2 Preprocessing

Raw EEG data underwent a standardized preprocessing pipeline implemented using the MNE-Python library [6]. All processing steps were applied consistently across all data segments:

- **Data Loading and Channel Selection:** Raw .edf files corresponding to the selected runs were loaded and concatenated (runs 4 and 8 for training, run 12 for over-time testing). Only EEG channels were retained for analysis, and a standard '10–05' montage was applied to ensure consistent electrode placement.
- **Filtering:** To allow individual feature extraction methods full control over frequency decomposition, no initial global bandpass filtering was applied to the raw EEG data, a common practice in BCI pipelines. Similarly, Common Average Reference (CAR) was not applied to preserve the intrinsic information of each sensor.
- **Epoching:** The continuous data was segmented into discrete trials, or "epochs," time-locked to the onset of motor imagery cues. For training and offline evaluation, epochs spanned from 0.5 s to 3.5 s relative to the cue onset. For simulated online (over-time) classification, a broader epoch window from -1.0 s to 4.0 s relative to the cue onset was used to facilitate sliding window analysis across the entire MI trial and pre-cue baseline.
- **Bad Data Handling:** Epochs identified as containing significant artifacts (e.g., excessive noise or outliers) were automatically dropped based on maximum peak-to-peak signal amplitude. Subsequently, the number of remaining epochs for each motor imagery class was equalized to ensure a balanced dataset, preventing classifier bias towards a majority class. Four subjects (71, 22, 82, and 20) had a complete set of 15 trials per class after this step. For the remaining subjects, one trial per class was rejected. For the online evaluation, all subjects had one trial rejected per class. All data were processed using double-precision floating-point (float64).

3   Feature Extraction Scenarios

We investigated three distinct feature extraction strategies, each designed to transform the multi-channel EEG time-series data into a discriminative feature vector for classification.

3.1   Band Power

This method extracts frequency-domain features directly from the time series of individual EEG channels. All frequency band power calculations employed Welch's method with n_fft=128, fmin=1, fmax=60, and n_per_seg dynamically set to the window length. We used five distinct frequency bands for each channel, reflecting common EEG rhythms: Theta (4–7 Hz), Alpha (8–12 Hz), Low Beta (13–20 Hz), High Beta (20–30 Hz), and Gamma (30–45 Hz). For each channel, the mean power within each of these five frequency bands was computed from the raw and unfiltered time-series data, yielding five features per channel (5 bands per each 64 channels). These features were used for training individual channel classifiers (discussed below) and served as the initial feature pool for mRMR feature selection.

3.2   Filter Bank Common Spatial Patterns (FBCSP)

FBCSP is a powerful spatial-spectral feature extraction technique that applies bandpass filters to the EEG data and then uses Common Spatial Patterns (CSP) to create optimal spatial filters [2]. These filters maximize the variance between the two motor imagery classes within each specific frequency band. We applied five distinct 4 Hz bandwidth filters ranging from 8 Hz to 28 Hz. For each of these five filtered bands, a separate CSP algorithm was applied to generate four CSP components, employing Ledoit-Wolf regularization (reg=0.01) for robust covariance estimation. Finally, the logarithm of the variance (log-power) of the spatially filtered components was extracted, resulting in a set of 20 features (5 bands x 4 components/band).

3.3   Minimum Redundancy Maximum Relevance (mRMR) Feature Selection

mRMR is a feature selection method used to identify an optimal subset of features that are highly relevant to the classification task while exhibiting minimal redundancy among themselves [12]. We utilized the Band Power features (mean power in the Theta, Alpha, Low Beta, High Beta, and Gamma bands) extracted from each individual EEG channel. For the 64-channel setup, this provided an initial feature space of 320 features (64 channels x 5 bands). The mRMR method was then applied to this entire 320-feature pool to select the top 20 features based on mutual information as both relevance and redundancy criteria.

4   Classification

We evaluated four widely used BCI classifiers [10], namely, Support Vector Machine (SVM), Multilayer Perceptron (MLP), K-Nearest Neighbors (KNN), and Linear Discriminant Analysis (LDA). These also served as base classifiers for the ensemble methods (Stacking and Majority Vote). For all base classifiers, hyperparameters were optimized using GridSearchCV with 5-fold StratifiedK-Fold cross-validation.

The base classifiers were trained distinctly for each feature extraction method. Thus, each base classifier was trained using the 20 globally mRMR-selected features and the 20 FBCSP features separately. For the Band Power features, we adopted a novel approach by creating individual channel classifiers, resulting in a total of 256 classifiers (4 classifier types x 64 channels). Subsequently, we selected the 10 best-performing individual channel classifiers (based on cross-validation accuracy) to serve as base classifiers for the Stacking and Majority Vote ensemble methods. Specifically, Majority Vote combines predictions by taking a simple majority vote among its base classifiers. Stacking, on the other hand, is a two-layer ensemble method. First, the base classifiers generate predictions. Second, a "meta-classifier" (in our case, an MLP with hyperparameters tuned via GridSearchCV) uses these predictions as new features and learns the optimal way to combine them into a final prediction.

We integrated the feature extraction and classification stages into a Sci-kit learn Pipeline for streamlined deployment. This was done separately for each individual channel classifier and for each full-array classifier type (FBCSP, mRMR). To prepare models for simulated real-time use, the final versions of all classifiers were trained on the entire dataset from the training runs (runs 4 and 8), leveraging the maximum available training data with optimal hyperparameters determined during offline evaluation. All final trained models were serialized and saved for subsequent loading and over-time evaluation.

Finally, a completely unseen EEG run (run 12) was used to simulate a real-time BCI setting. A fixed-duration sliding window of 0.5 s moved across the test data epochs with a step size of 0.1 s. Each of the final "online" classifiers (Stacking, Majority Vote, FBCSP-based, mRMR-based, and the 10 best individual channel classifiers) predicted the data within this window. For each complete pipeline, we recorded the classification accuracy and the prediction time (time taken for the model to process a single window, in milliseconds). Figure 1 summarizes the entire experimental setup, which was conducted on a Windows 11 Dell Precision 3680 Tower CTO Base, equipped with an Intel® Core™ i9 14900K processor (24 Cores, 6.0 GHz Turbo, 125 W), 32GB RAM (2 × 16 GB, DDR5, 4400 MT/s, non-ECC), a 1 TB SSD, and no GPU configuration.

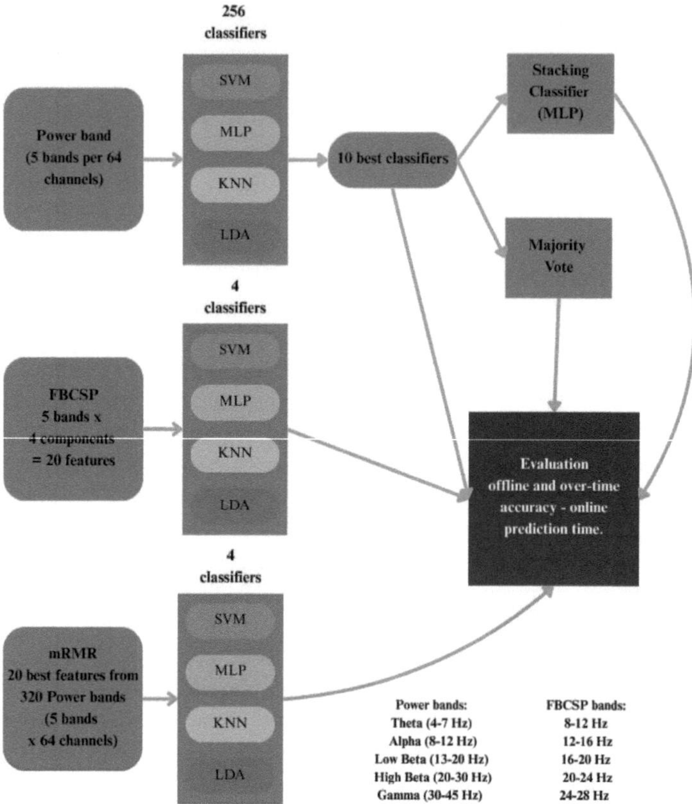

Fig. 1. Experimental evaluation: proposed power band individual channel classifiers compared against established channel space dimension reduction (FBCSP), and feature selection methods (mRMR). Base classifiers are trained individually for each feature extraction method. Ensemble methods trained from the 10-best classifiers from the individual pool (256 models, 4 classifiers per each individual channel). Evaluation carried out in offline and over-time accuracy and time prediction (for online only).

5   Results

Our findings are presented in three distinct stages: i) an exhaustive analysis of all individual channel classifiers; ii) an evaluation of the top-performing 10-best individual channel classifiers; and iii) a simulated over-time classification performance assessment. For each stage, we quantify the average classification accuracy across subjects, individual classifiers, and specific channels. The performance of the proposed individual and ensemble classifiers is systematically compared against established methods, specifically Filter Bank Common Spatial Pattern (FBCSP) and Minimum Redundancy Maximum Relevance (mRMR) with their respective base classifiers.

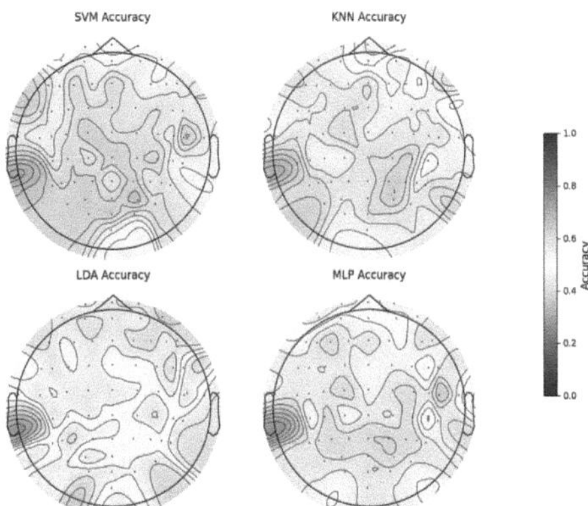

Fig. 2. Topographical distribution of individual channel accuracies averaged across subjects. Blue areas represent accuracy above chance level (0.5). Accuracies reported from the training data under stratified 5-fold cross-validation. (Color figure online)

5.1   Performance of All Individual Classifiers

Initial insights into the topographical distribution of accuracy, averaged across subjects for all individual classifiers, are presented in Fig. 2. This visualization highlights that electrodes positioned over the left temporal and central cortices consistently yield higher classification accuracies, exceeding chance level. Specifically, the K-Nearest Neighbors (KNN), Support Vector Machine (SVM), and Multilayer Perceptron (MLP) classifiers demonstrate robust performance on central electrodes, forming a distinct high-accuracy distribution over the motor cortex, consistent with known brain regions involved in motor imagery (MI).

The aggregated classification accuracies across subjects for all individual channel classifiers are depicted in Fig. 3. A notable inter-subject variability is observed, with at least three out of ten participants performing around or below the chance level (0.5). The mean accuracy per subject ranges from a maximum of 0.64 ± 0.08 to a minimum of 0.44 ± 0.09, with an overall mean and standard error of the mean (SEM) of 0.53 ± 0.08. When comparing across different methodologies, the mRMR method, particularly with CSP and KNN, demonstrably overperforms other methods and classifiers, achieving an accuracy of 0.78. This is followed by the Stacking ensemble, with 0.67. Conversely, the Majority Vote ensemble failed to reach an accuracy above the chance level. Classifiers utilizing the CSP method generally performed around 0.55, except for LDA, which exhibited chance-level accuracy. Interestingly, three subjects achieved accuracies surpassing the average CSP method performance, and one additional subject matched it.

Further examining the performance across base classifiers within the individual channel setup, Fig. 4 illustrates the mean accuracy for each of the four classifier types. SVM demonstrated superior performance with a mean accuracy of 0.57, outperforming the average of CSP methods. KNN and MLP achieved

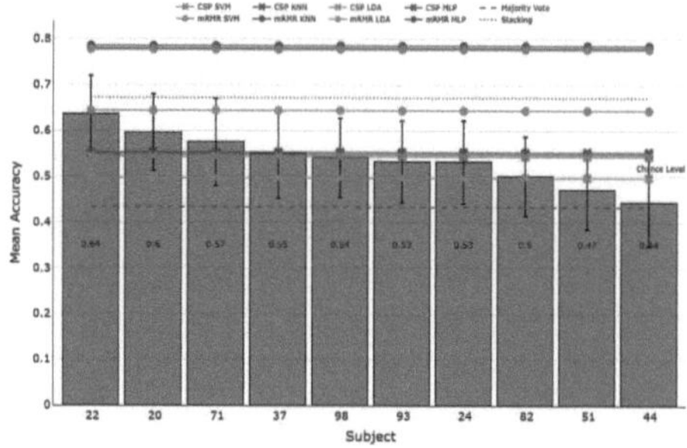

Fig. 3. Mean accuracy per subject for individual channel classifiers. Lines represent feature extraction methods (CSP: cross-marked; mRMR: circle-marked) and ensemble methods (Majority Vote: red dotted; Stacking: blue dashed). Chance level is at 0.5. Accuracies reported from the training data under stratified 5-fold cross-validation. (Color figure online)

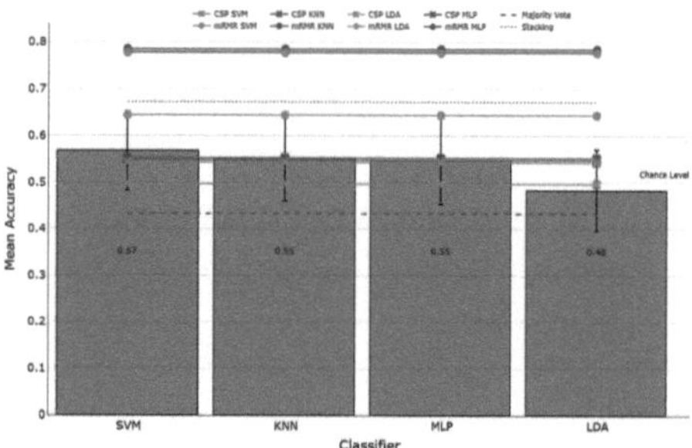

Fig. 4. Mean accuracy per classifier for individual channel classifiers. Lines represent feature extraction methods (CSP: cross-marked; mRMR: circle-marked) and ensemble methods (Majority Vote: red dotted; Stacking: blue dashed). Chance level is at 0.5. Accuracies reported from the training data under stratified 5-fold cross-validation. (Color figure online)

similar accuracies of 0.55, while LDA also managed to perform above chance level. This observed trend aligns with the topographical distribution shown in Fig. 2, where SVM contributes more prominently to the blue (higher accuracy) regions. Overall, the mean accuracy across all classifiers in this individual channel setup was 0.537 ± 0.089.

Figure 5 presents a channel-specific analysis of achieved accuracy. Out of 64 channels, nine (CP6, F2, FP1, F4, AF7, AFz, AF8, FP2, Fpz) exhibited performance at or above the chance level (0.5). Furthermore, a substantial subset of 19 channels (POz, Pz, O1, P4, CP2, PO8, P7, CPz, C1, P1, PO7, Oz, P5, P2, P3, CP4, T8, PO4, TP7) individually outperformed the CSP classifiers, with accuracies ranging from 0.56 ± 0.08 to 0.62 ± 0.09, and an average of 0.537 ± 0.089. Consistent with the topographical distribution observed in Fig. 2, channels

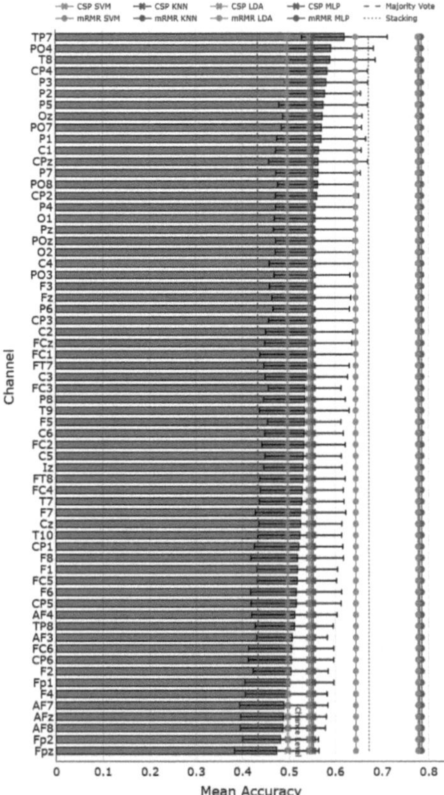

Fig. 5. Mean accuracy per channel for individual channel classifiers. Lines represent feature extraction methods (CSP: cross-marked; mRMR: circle-marked) and ensemble methods (Majority Vote: red dotted; Stacking: blue dashed). Chance level is at 0.5. Accuracies reported from the training data under stratified 5-fold cross-validation. (Color figure online)

located in the temporal, posterior, central, and occipital regions demonstrated the highest accuracies.

5.2 Performance of the 10-Best Individual Classifiers

From the initial pool of 256 individual channel classifiers, we identified the 10 best-performing classifiers for each subject, resulting in a consolidated pool of 100 top classifiers. A comparative analysis of the accuracies from the 10 best and 10 worst individual channel and classifier combinations per subject within this consolidated pool is presented in Fig. 6. The accuracies for the 10 worst-performing classifiers range from 0.65 ± 0.10 to 0.79 ± 0.10, while the 10 best-performing classifiers achieve accuracies between 0.69 ± 0.06 and 0.90 ± 0.06. This significant improvement demonstrates that filtering for the top 10 classifiers per subject yields a selection of models that consistently and substantially outperform chance level. Notably, the group of 10 best classifiers from our proposed individual channel approach outperforms the mRMR classifiers, and even the 10 worst-performing classifiers within this selected group exceed the accuracies obtained by the FBCSP classifiers. These findings underscore the efficacy of our proposed individual channel classification strategy in developing highly effective BCI classifiers.

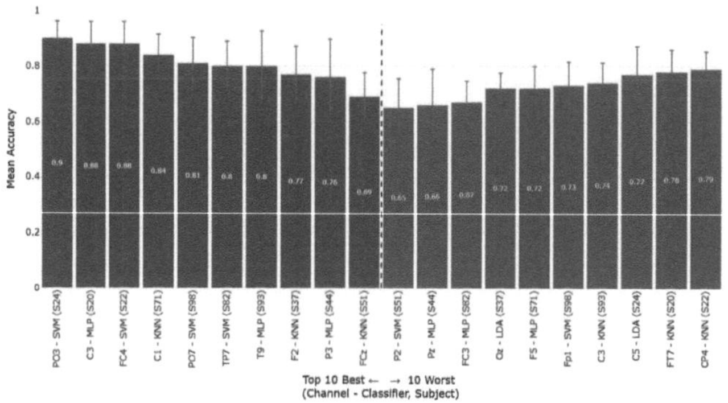

Fig. 6. Performance distribution of the 10 best and 10 worst channel-classifier combinations for each subject, derived from the original 256 individual channel classifiers. Groups are demarcated by a vertical dotted line and color-coding.

To gain a more granular understanding of the most influential channels, classifiers, and their combinations within the 100 best classifiers pool, we performed a statistical analysis, where Fig. 7a illustrates the most frequently utilized individual channels. Posterior channels were most prominent, appearing 18 times, followed by temporal channels (10 times). Central and occipital channels were each selected 7 times. This distribution is consistent with the topographical result (Fig. 2, highlighting the importance of these regions for MI-BCI). Regarding classifier preference within this top-performing pool, Fig. 7b reveals that SVM was the most frequently used classifier (41 times), followed by MLP (28 times), KNN (20 times), and LDA (11 times). This indicates a strong preference for SVM in achieving high individual channel classification accuracies.

The analysis of channel and classifier combinations, presented in Fig. 7c, yields interesting insights. Surprisingly, the occipital channel O2 combined with KNN was the most frequent pairing, appearing three times among the 100 best individual channel-classifier models. Several other combinations appeared twice, including SVM with central (CPz), temporal (T9, T8), and posterior (PO3, P7) channels; MLP with temporal (T8) and posterior (Pz) channels; and TP7 for LDA and PO4 for KNN. These findings suggest that the typical lateralization observed in the motor cortex (e.g., C3 and C4) for motor imagery can be extended to encompass informative contributions from temporal (T8, T9) and occipital/posterior (PO3, PO4) brain regions. This broadens the conventional understanding of critical channel locations in MI-BCI.

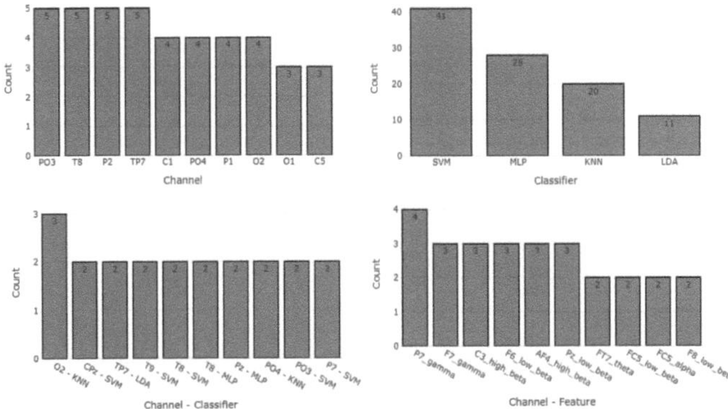

Fig. 7. Statistical distribution of selected components from the 100 best classifiers pool: (a) most frequently used individual channels, (b) most frequently used classifiers, (c) most frequent channel and classifier combinations. (d) Most frequently selected features by the mRMR method (channel and power band combination).

Finally, Fig. 7d presents the most frequently selected features by the mRMR method, combining individual channels with specific power bands. The posterior channel P7, coupled with the gamma band, emerged as the most frequently used feature. This was followed by features from frontal and central regions, predominantly associated with beta bands (high and low), including the expected C3 high beta rhythm, which is typically related to sensorimotor rhythms. Interestingly, the alpha band was only selected for the FC5 channel. The use of the mRMR approach provides valuable information regarding both the brain areas and the frequency bands from which the most discriminative features originate.

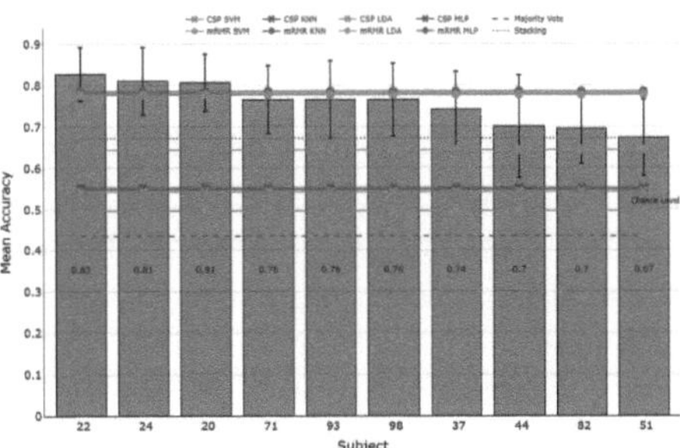

Fig. 8. Mean accuracy per subject for the 10-best individual channel classifiers. Lines represent feature extraction methods (CSP: cross-marked; mRMR: circle-marked) and ensemble methods (Majority Vote: red dotted; Stacking: blue dashed). Chance level is at 0.5. Accuracies reported from the training data under stratified 5-fold cross-validation. (Color figure online)

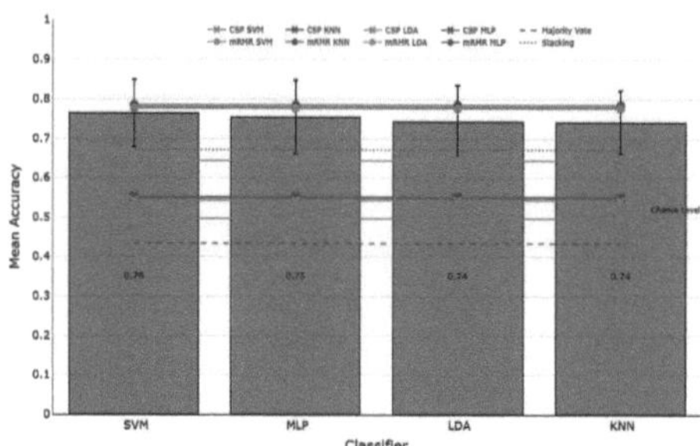

Fig. 9. Mean accuracy per classifier for 10-best individual channel classifiers. Lines represent feature extraction methods (CSP: cross-marked; mRMR: circle-marked) and ensemble methods (Majority Vote: red dotted; Stacking: blue dashed). Chance level is at 0.5. Accuracies reported from the training data under stratified 5-fold cross-validation. (Color figure online)

Continuing with the previous analysis, we re-evaluated the mean classification accuracy across subjects (Fig. 8), classifiers (Fig. 9), and channels (Fig. 10), based on the subset of 10 best-performing individual channel classifiers per subject. A notable improvement in accuracy was observed across all subjects, with the overall mean accuracy per subject reaching 0.754 ± 0.087. This represents an improvement of at least 20% compared to the full pool of individual classifiers. The mean accuracy per subject ranged from a minimum of 0.67 ± 0.09 to a maximum of 0.83 ± 0.06. All subjects achieved higher accuracies than those obtained with the FBCSP method. Furthermore, three subjects (IDs 22, 24, 20) demonstrated performance superior to both the mRMR and FBCSP feature extraction methods, as well as the ensemble classifiers. These results suggest that selecting only the 10 best individual channel classifiers for each subject significantly enhances overall classification accuracy.

Consistent with the subject-specific improvements, the mean accuracy per classifier also demonstrated a substantial increase. The four base classifiers (SVM, MLP, LDA, and KNN) achieved a consistent average accuracy of 0.75 ± 0.08, effectively narrowing the initial 0.09 accuracy gap observed between SVM and LDA in the full classifier pool. Among these, SVM maintained the highest mean accuracy at 0.76 ± 0.08, indicating its robust performance across the experimental conditions.

In the channel-specific analysis of the 10-best classifiers, 13 out of 64 channels (FT7, T10, CP4, T9, C6, F3, FC2, PO3, C3, CP3, P4, F1, FC4) exhibited accuracies ranging from 0.79 ± 0.03 to 0.88 ± 0.08, with a mean average of 0.75 ± 0.08. This represents a 20% improvement in average accuracy compared to the full-channel analysis. All these channels consistently outperformed all feature extraction methods and ensemble classifiers. Mirroring earlier findings, channels in the posterior, temporal, and central cortices continued to yield the highest accuracies. Notably, the frontal cortex also contributed to this improved

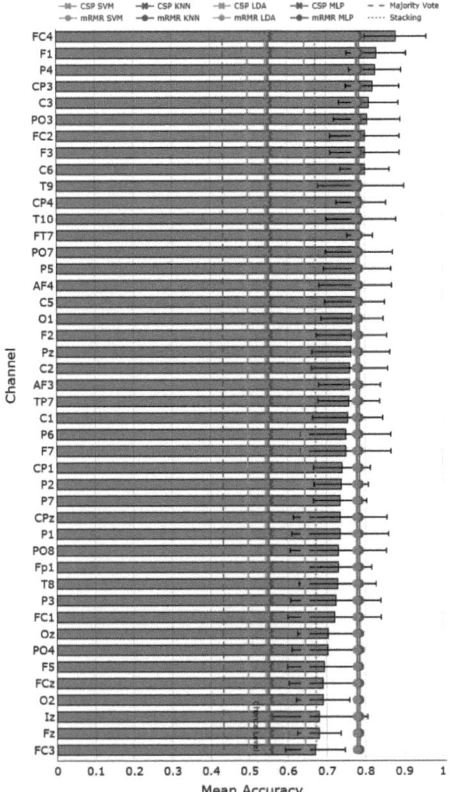

Fig. 10. Mean accuracy per channel for 10-best individual channel classifiers. Lines represent feature extraction methods (CSP: cross-marked; mRMR: circle-marked) and ensemble methods (Majority Vote: red dotted; Stacking: blue dashed). Chance level is at 0.5. Accuracies reported from the training data under stratified 5-fold cross-validation. (Color figure online)

performance metric, suggesting its relevance within the selected optimal channel subsets.

5.3   Over-Time Classification

To validate our individual channel classifier proposal, we conducted an over-time classification using unseen data, simulating an online BCI scenario. Figure 11 presents the over-time accuracy heatmap, where blue indicates higher accuracy, white represents chance level, and red denotes below-chance performance. As is common in BCI, achieving high accuracies in online prediction remains challenging, and significant variability is expected in the timing of peak performance, reflecting the dynamic and sensitive nature of brain signals. Therefore, certain subjects (98, 51, 20) demonstrated high accuracies during the late

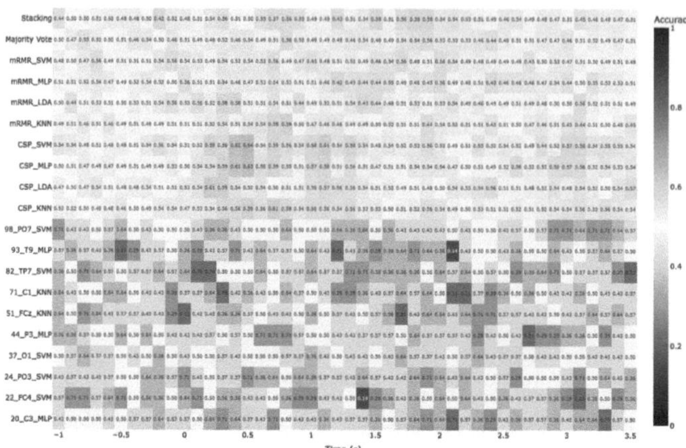

Fig. 11. Classification rates over time for unseen data. The X-axis represents the time from cue onset (0 s), while the Y-axis lists the best individual channel classifier per subject, the base classifiers for each extraction method, and ensemble classifiers. The sliding window duration is 0.5 s, with a step size of 0.1 s.

stages of the epoch (3.0 to 3.5 s), while others (20, 24, 44, 71, 93) achieved peak performance in the middle (1.5 to 2.0 s), and some (20, 71, 82, 44) performed well at the beginning (0 to 1.0 s). For the mRMR and ensemble classifiers, the time window with above-chance level accuracy typically fell between 1.5 and 2.0 s. Intriguingly, FBCSP classifiers consistently maintained performance close to 0.5 and showed improved accuracies towards the end of the epoch (near 3.5 s). However, the individual channel classifiers exhibited higher variability below the chance level compared to other methods, suggesting that while they can achieve high peak accuracies, their overall stability for continuous online prediction might be lower.

A critical factor for online BCI systems is the computational time required for feature extraction and classification. We quantified the mean prediction time for each pipeline (feature extraction + classifier) per window, as presented in Table 1. FBCSP methods incur longer prediction times (more than double) compared to other methods, followed by mRMR and ensemble classifiers. In contrast, all individual channel classifiers achieved considerably faster prediction times, consistently under 4 milliseconds. This substantial temporal advantage arises from the fundamental difference in approach: FBCSP and mRMR process data from the full array of channels for feature extraction before classification, whereas the individual channel approach is highly focused, requiring only the calculation of band power from a single, specific electrode. This highlights a key practical benefit of our proposed method for real-time BCI applications.

Table 1. Mean prediction times (ms) for various classifiers per window, using a 0.5-s sliding window with 0.1-s step size.

Classifier	Mean prediction time (ms)
FBCSP KNN	53.390922
FBCSP MLP	42.967157
FBCSP SVM	41.339242
FBCSP LDA	41.036424
mRMR KNN	23.805141
Stacking	21.132737
Majority Vote	19.531575
mRMR SVM	10.236262
mRMR LDA	9.556881
mRMR MLP	8.680306
P3 MLP	3.283138
C1 KNN	2.970162
PO7 SVM	2.723533
FCz KNN	2.560875
FC4 SVM	1.819756
PO3 SVM	1.736631
O1 SVM	1.655677
TP7 SVM	1.468513
C3 MLP	1.271289
T9 MLP	1.206880

6   Discussion and Conclusions

This study investigated a novel approach to improve Motor Imagery Brain-Computer Interface (MI-BCI) classification rates by training individual channel classifiers rather than utilizing the full electrode array. Our methodology involved evaluating this approach in both offline and pseudo-online settings, using unseen data for over-time prediction, recreating a real-time scenario. We benchmarked individual channel performance, along with ensemble classifiers (Stacking and Majority Vote), against two established feature extraction methods: minimum Redundancy Maximum Relevance (mRMR) and Filter Bank Common Spatial Patterns (FBCSP). Feature extraction relied on power bands within Theta (4–7 Hz), Alpha (8–12 Hz), Beta (13–20 Hz and 20–30 Hz), and Gamma (30–45 Hz) frequency ranges. Support Vector Machine (SVM), K-Nearest Neighbors (KNN), Linear Discriminant Analysis (LDA), and Multi-Layer Perceptron (MLP) served as base classifiers, hyperparameterized and trained via stratified 5-fold cross-validation (see Fig. 1 for a summary).

Initially, the full pool of individual channel classifiers (256 per subject: 4 classifiers × 64 channels) exhibited suboptimal performance, with three subjects performing below chance level and only three outperforming the FBCSP approach. This underperformance relative to mRMR and a stacking classifier underscores the well-established efficacy of data engineering techniques in optimizing feature selection for high classification accuracy. Interestingly, the most frequently selected features within our individual channel approach diverged from typical MI-BCI findings; only C3 in the high Beta band was consistently observed, while P7 and F7 gamma features led the ranking. This prominent left-hemisphere activity suggests that P7 low gamma (30–45 Hz) may reflect the spatial, kinesthetic, and sensory-integrative aspects of imagined movement within internal motor models, while F7 low gamma may indicate the active engagement of frontal executive functions related to motor planning and inhibition [8]. However, the interpretation of 30–45 Hz gamma on scalp EEG necessitates extreme caution due to pervasive muscle artifact contamination, particularly in frontal and temporal regions [5]. As our primary focus was BCI classification, exhaustive Independent Component Analysis (ICA) for muscle artifact extraction was not performed in this preliminary phase.

When we refined our approach by selecting the top-10 best-performing individual channel classifiers per subject, classification accuracies significantly improved by approximately 20%. Notably, at least three subjects then outperformed mRMR, and all subjects achieved accuracies superior to 0.67%, surpassing FBCSP. These results suggest that focusing on a curated subset of high-performing individual channel classifiers, potentially within specific regions of interest, can reduce inter- and intra-subject variability and yield superior performance compared to using a full electrode array. This approach presents a novel alternative to traditional optimization-based channel selection. Our findings resonate with recent work, such as that by Soler et al. [18,19], who demonstrated that individualized channel subsets, even if asymmetrical and not conforming to standard electrode distributions, can achieve superior classification accuracy. This further supports the utility of incorporating areas beyond the classical motor cortex, including temporal, parietal, frontal, and even occipital regions (though occipital activity may be more related to visual stimuli), in personalized BCI arrays. Future research should meticulously investigate the specific roles of these diverse brain regions in BCI to enhance accuracy and reduce variability through customized electrode configurations, potentially leveraging higher spatial sampling from broader head coverage, including cerebellar regions, to advance the current state of the art.

The methodology employed herein offers a unique framework for evaluating the contribution of individual channels in MI-BCI. While FBCSP relies on global spatial filters across multiple frequency bands, and mRMR selects a global subset of channel-band combinations, our individual channel approach, by focusing on localized band power, may capture distinct discriminative information. To leverage this, we integrated ensemble classifiers, where the novelty lies in constructing an ensemble from these individual channel classifiers, a departure from traditional ensembles trained on the same feature set. Although the Majority Vote ensemble did not consistently improve predictions, the stacking classifier, utilizing a meta-learner, consistently yielded high accuracies, even in over-time prediction, where individual classifiers exhibited significant variability.

This individual channel classification framework holds promise for informing channel selection before applying global spatial filtering techniques like CSP, potentially leading to more stable classifiers over time. An intriguing extension of this approach would be its application to dynamic, adaptive channel selection in real-time BCI systems. Given the low latency achievable by individual classifiers, this could facilitate continuous optimization of channel subsets, which may vary within or across sessions, thereby improving the robustness and adaptability of MI-BCI.

Acknowledgments. First author wants to thank Fabien Lotte for his valuable views and suggestions in the experimental section of this paper.

Disclosure of Interests. The authors have no competing interests to declare that are relevant to the content of this article.

References

1. Abdullah, Faye, I., Islam, M.R.: Eeg channel selection techniques in motor imagery applications: a review and new perspectives. Bioengineering **9**(12), 726 (2022)
2. Ang, K.K., Chin, Z.Y., Zhang, H., Guan, C.: Filter bank common spatial pattern (fbcsp) in brain-computer interface. In: 2008 IEEE International Joint Conference on Neural Networks (IEEE World Congress on Computational Intelligence), pp. 2390–2397. IEEE (2008)
3. Bonnet, L., Lotte, F., Lécuyer, A.: Two brains, one game: design and evaluation of a multiuser bci video game based on motor imagery. IEEE Trans. Comput. Intell. AI Games **5**(2), 185–198 (2013)
4. Frølich, L., Winkler, I., Müller, K.R., Samek, W.: Investigating effects of different artefact types on motor imagery bci. In: 2015 37th Annual International Conference of the IEEE Engineering in Medicine and Biology Society (EMBC), pp. 1942–1945. IEEE (2015)
5. Goncharova, I.I., McFarland, D.J., Vaughan, T.M., Wolpaw, J.R.: Emg contamination of eeg: spectral and topographical characteristics. Clin. Neurophysiol. **114**(9), 1580–1593 (2003)
6. Gramfort, A., et al.: Mne software for processing meg and eeg data. Neuroimage **86**, 446–460 (2014)
7. Javidan, M., Yazdchi, M., Baharlouei, Z., Mahnam, A.: Feature and channel selection for designing a regression-based continuous-variable emotion recognition system with two eeg channels. Biomed. Signal Process. Control **70**, 102979 (2021)
8. Khan, Y.U., Sepulveda, F.: Brain-computer interface for single-trial eeg classification for wrist movement imagery using spatial filtering in the gamma band. IET Signal Proc. **4**(5), 510–517 (2010)
9. Lin, C.L., Chen, L.T.: Improvement of brain–computer interface in motor imagery training through the designing of a dynamic experiment and fbcsp. Heliyon **9**(3) (2023)

10. Lotte, F., et al.: A review of classification algorithms for eeg-based brain-computer interfaces: a 10 year update. J. Neural Eng. **15**(3), 031005 (2018)
11. Neuper, C., Scherer, R., Wriessnegger, S., Pfurtscheller, G.: Motor imagery and action observation: modulation of sensorimotor brain rhythms during mental control of a brain-computer interface. Clin. Neurophysiol. **120**(2), 239–247 (2009)
12. Peng, H., Long, F., Ding, C.: Feature selection based on mutual information criteria of max-dependency, max-relevance, and min-redundancy. IEEE Trans. Pattern Anal. Mach. Intell. **27**(8), 1226–1238 (2005)
13. Pfurtscheller, G., Neuper, C.: Motor imagery activates primary sensorimotor area in humans. Neurosci. Lett. **239**(2–3), 65–68 (1997)
14. Riascos, J., Molinas, M., Lotte, F.: Machine learning methods for bci: challenges, pitfalls and promises. In: ESANN 2024-European Symposium on Artificial Neural Networks, Computational Intelligence and Machine Learning (2024)
15. Riascos, J., Villa, S., Maciel, A., Nedel, L., Barone, D.: Towards moving virtual arms using brain-computer interface. In: Computer Graphics International Conference, pp. 445–452. Springer (2019)
16. Schalk, G., McFarland, D.J., Hinterberger, T., Birbaumer, N., Wolpaw, J.R.: Bci 2000: a general-purpose brain-computer interface (bci) system. IEEE Trans. Biomed. Eng. **51**(6), 1034–1043 (2004)
17. Shuqfa, Z., Lakas, A., Belkacem, A.N.: Increasing accessibility to a large brain-computer interface dataset: curation of physionet eeg motor movement/imagery dataset for decoding and classification. Data Brief **54**, 110181 (2024)
18. Soler, A., Giraldo, E., Molinas, M.: Eeg source imaging of hand movement-related areas: an evaluation of the reconstruction and classification accuracy with optimized channels. Brain Inf. **11**(1), 11 (2024)
19. Soler, A., Moctezuma, L.A., Giraldo, E., Molinas, M.: Automated methodology for optimal selection of minimum electrode subsets for accurate eeg source estimation based on genetic algorithm optimization. Sci. Rep. **12**(1), 11221 (2022)
20. Thomas, K.P., Guan, C., Lau, C.T., Vinod, A.P., Ang, K.K.: A new discriminative common spatial pattern method for motor imagery brain-computer interfaces. IEEE Trans. Biomed. Eng. **56**(11), 2730–2733 (2009)
21. Tzdaka, E., Benaroch, C., Jeunet, C., Lotte, F.: Assessing the relevance of neurophysiological patterns to predict motor imagery-based bci users' performance. In: 2020 IEEE International Conference on Systems, Man, and Cybernetics (SMC), pp. 2490–2495. IEEE (2020)
22. Wang, X., Lu, H., Shen, X., Ma, L., Wang, Y.: Prosthetic control system based on motor imagery. Comput. Methods Biomech. Biomed. Engin. **25**(7), 764–771 (2022)
23. Wolpaw, J.R., Millán, J.d.R., Ramsey, N.F.: Brain-computer interfaces: definitions and principles. Handbook Clin. Neurol. **168**, 15–23 (2020)
24. Yu, Y., et al.: Self-paced operation of a wheelchair based on a hybrid brain-computer interface combining motor imagery and p300 potential. IEEE Trans. Neural Syst. Rehabil. Eng. **25**(12), 2516–2526 (2017)
25. Zapała, D., et al.: The effects of handedness on sensorimotor rhythm desynchronization and motor-imagery bci control. Sci. Rep. **10**(1), 2087 (2020)

Hemispheric-Specific Coupling Improves Modeling of Functional Connectivity Using Wilson–Cowan Dynamics

Ramiro Plüss[1], Hernán Villota[2(✉)], and Patricio Orio[3,4]

[1] Instituto Tecnológico de Buenos Aires (ITBA), CABA, Argentina
`rpluss@itba.edu.ar`
[2] Institución Universitaria de Envigado (IUE), Envigado, Colombia
`hdvillota@correo.iue.edu.co`
[3] Insituto de Neurociencias, Facultad de Ciencias, Universidad de Valparaíso, Valparaíso, Chile
`patricio.orio@uv.cl`
[4] Centro Interdisciplinario de Neurociencia de Valparaíso, Universidad de Valparaíso, Valparaíso, Chile

Abstract. Large-scale neural mass models have been widely used to simulate resting-state brain activity from structural connectivity. In this work, we extend a well-established Wilson–Cowan framework by introducing a novel hemispheric-specific coupling scheme that differentiates between intra-hemispheric and inter-hemispheric structural interactions. We apply this model to empirical cortical connectomes and resting-state fMRI data from matched control and schizophrenia groups. Simulated functional connectivity is computed from the band-limited envelope correlations of regional excitatory activity and compared against empirical functional connectivity matrices. Our results show that incorporating hemispheric asymmetries enhances the correlation between simulated and empirical functional connectivity, highlighting the importance of anatomically-informed coupling strategies in improving the biological realism of large-scale brain network models.

Keywords: Wilson–Cowan model · structural connectivity · functional connectivity · schizophrenia · neural dynamics · hemispheric coupling

1 Introduction

Schizophrenia is a severe neuropsychiatric disorder characterized by profound disruptions in thought processes, perception, and affect regulation. Mounting evidence indicates that these symptoms are associated with altered functional connectivity (FC) across large-scale brain networks, particularly within and between the default mode, frontoparietal control, and salience networks [10,13]. Understanding how these functional abnormalities arise from the underlying anatomical organization, or structural connectivity (SC), remains a central question in computational psychiatry. Structural connectomes derived from diffusion MRI provide a static scaffold upon which neural dynamics unfold. However, the mapping between SC and FC is complex due to nonlinear interactions and modulatory processes that shape brain activity. Computational models of whole-brain dynamics offer a principled framework to investigate this SC–FC relationship. In particular, the Wilson–Cowan neural mass model provides a biologically grounded formalism to simulate excitatory and inhibitory population dynamics, enabling the generation of realistic large-scale activity patterns [1,2]. In this work, we simulate FC from empirical cortical SC matrices obtained from matched control and schizophrenia groups. To isolate cortical dynamics and minimize confounds related to deep nuclei, we restrict our analysis to cortical regions. We first implement a classic whole-brain model with uniform global coupling strength (G), and then introduce a novel hemispheric-specific coupling strategy that distinguishes intra- (G_1) and inter-hemispheric (G_2) connectivity. This extension is motivated by anatomical and functional asymmetries previously reported in both healthy and clinical populations [10]. We evaluate the capacity of each model variant to reproduce empirical resting-state FC, using Pearson correlation as a measure of SC–FC correspondence. Additionally, we analyze group differences and explore the role of hemispheric specificity in capturing altered integration patterns observed in schizophrenia. Our results show that introducing hemispheric coupling parameters improves the model's performance and may help reveal biologically meaningful asymmetries in large-scale brain dynamics.

2   Material and Methods

2.1   Empirical Dataset and Brain Network Estimation

We employed a publicly available dataset containing diffusion and functional MRI scans from 27 patients with schizophrenia and 27 demographically matched healthy controls [13,14]. These data were acquired using a 3T Siemens Trio scanner and include high-resolution T1-weighted images, diffusion spectrum imaging (DSI), and resting-state fMRI. Participants in the patient group met DSM-IV criteria for schizophrenia or schizoaffective disorder, and were recruited from the Lausanne University Hospital. Brain network construction was performed using the Connectome Mapping Toolkit [6]. Cortical segmentation was based on the Lausanne 2008 multi-scale parcellation scheme [7], from which we selected the 83-region resolution to balance anatomical specificity with computational feasibility. SC matrices were derived from deterministic streamline tractography applied to the DSI data, with edge weights defined as normalized streamline counts accounting for surface area and length biases [3]. FC was estimated as the absolute Pearson correlation between regional mean BOLD signals after standard preprocessing, including motion correction, nuisance regression, spatial smoothing, and band-pass filtering [4,11]. This framework provides subject-level structural and functional networks with matched parcellations, enabling direct comparison and simulation of brain dynamics constrained by individual connectomes. To reduce inter-subject variability and highlight group-level trends, we computed group-average SC and FC matrices separately for the control (CTRL) and schizophrenia (SCHZ) cohorts. Since all individual SC and FC matrices are symmetric by construction, owing to the undirected nature of tractography and the use of Pearson correlation, the resulting group-average matrices are also symmetric. This approach allows us to focus on global network properties and systematic differences between groups, rather than individual-specific fluctuations. By simulating neural dynamics on the group-averaged SC using the Wilson–Cowan model, we can directly assess how alterations in anatomical connectivity influence the emergence of functional interactions at the population level. Furthermore, the use of averaged matrices facilitates a controlled exploration of model parameters, such as global versus hemispheric-specific coupling schemes, enabling us to investigate how different modes of interaction (intra-hemispheric vs. inter-hemispheric connectivity) affect the model's ability to reproduce empirical FC. This is particularly relevant in schizophrenia, where disruptions in inter-hemispheric integration have been consistently reported. Finally, from a translational perspective, the group-level SC and FC matrices serve as clinical reference profiles, against which deviations at the individual level could be later evaluated. This provides a meaningful scaffold for assessing the impact of pathological alterations and testing hypotheses about network-level mechanisms underlying psychiatric disorders. The 83-region resolution includes both cortical and subcortical structures. To restrict the analysis to cortical dynamics, we excluded subcortical regions and the brainstem, resulting in 68 cortical ROIs (34 per hemisphere). This reduction ensures compatibility with the Wilson–Cowan neural mass model, which is defined at the mesoscopic cortical level. All modeling and simulation steps were performed on these 68×68 group-average matrices.

2.2 Wilson–Cowan Network Model

We employed a whole-brain neural mass model based on the Wilson–Cowan equations [1,2], which describe the dynamics of coupled excitatory (E) and inhibitory (I) neural populations. Each cortical region k is modeled as a pair of interacting populations governed by Eq. (1) and Eq. (2).

$$\tau_e \frac{dE_k}{dt} = -E_k + (1 - r_e E_k) S_e \left(a_{ee} E_k - a_{ei,k} I_k + G \sum_{\substack{l=1 \\ l \neq k}}^{N} C_{kl} E_l + P \right) \tag{1}$$

$$\tau_i \frac{dI_k}{dt} = -I_k + (1 - r_i I_k) S_i \left(a_{ie} E_k - a_{ii} I_k + Q \right) \tag{2}$$

Here, τ_e and τ_i are the time constants for excitatory and inhibitory populations, respectively; r_e and r_i modulate population refractoriness; and $a_{\alpha\beta}$ are synaptic weight parameters. The matrix C_{kl} encodes the normalized structural connectivity between regions, and G is a global coupling parameter. P and Q represent constant external inputs. The transfer function $S(x; \mu, \sigma)$ is a sigmoidal non-linearity that governs the population response, where μ defines the activation threshold and σ controls the slope of the transition. Its general form is given by Eq. (3).

$$S(x) = \frac{1}{1 + \exp\left(-\frac{x-\mu}{\sigma}\right)} \tag{3}$$

This formulation has been widely used to simulate large-scale brain dynamics and to investigate the emergence of functional connectivity from anatomical structure [8]. To derive the simulated FC, we followed a standard pipeline: (I) we extracted the excitatory activity $E_k(t)$ from each cortical region after a transient period; (II) each time series was band-pass filtered in the 0.01–0.1 Hz range to match the frequency content of resting-state BOLD fluctuations; (III) we computed the analytic signal using the Hilbert transform and obtained its amplitude envelope $A_k(t)$, which captures the slow modulation of neural activity; and (IV) the simulated FC matrix was defined as the Pearson correlation between all pairs of amplitude envelopes $\{A_k(t), A_j(t)\}$. This procedure follows standard methods for estimating resting-state FC from band-limited neural signals and ensures methodological consistency with the empirical FC derived from resting-state fMRI, allowing direct comparison between simulated and empirical connectivity matrices.

2.3   Inhibitory Synaptic Plasticity

To enhance the model's stability and biological plausibility, we adopt a inhibitory synaptic plasticity (ISP) mechanism [12]. This rule dynamically modulates the inhibitory-to-excitatory coupling $a_{ei}(t)$ within each cortical region based on local activity levels. The weight evolves according to Eq. (4).

$$\tau_p \frac{da_{ei}}{dt} = I(E - \rho_E) \tag{4}$$

The parameter τ_p is the adaptation time constant and ρ_E is a target excitatory level. This form of homeostatic ISP promotes balanced excitation-inhibition interactions, preventing runaway excitation and enabling sustained oscillatory activity across a wide range of coupling regimes. By integrating Eq. (4) alongside the Wilson–Cowan dynamics, the model remains compatible with empirical resting-state activity, while improving robustness and interpretability. Similar ISP rules have been shown to support biologically realistic network dynamics in large-scale simulations [8, 12].

2.4   Hemispheric-Specific Coupling

The standard formulation uses a single global parameter G to scale all long-range excitatory inputs. However, anatomical studies have shown that inter-hemispheric connections are sparser and more variable than intra-hemispheric ones, and that this asymmetry may be exaggerated in schizophrenia [10]. We introduce a modified coupling scheme that differentiates between intra- and inter-hemispheric projections via two parameters, G_1 and G_2, respectively. Figure 1 illustrates the difference between the global and hemispheric-specific coupling schemes applied to the structural connectivity matrix.

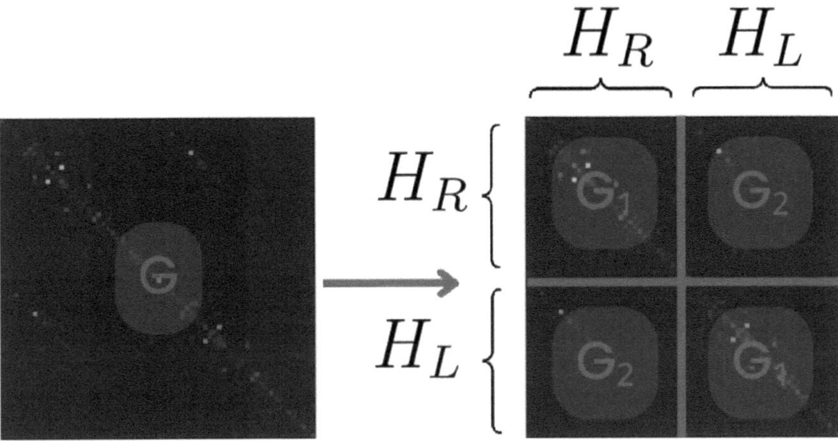

Fig. 1. Coupling schemes in the Wilson–Cowan model. The left panel illustrates global coupling using a single parameter G, which uniformly modulates connectivity across all regions. The right panel shows hemispheric-specific coupling, where G_1 modulates intra-hemispheric connections and G_2 modulates inter-hemispheric ones. The structural matrix is reordered such that the first 34 regions correspond to the right hemisphere (H_R) and the last 34 to the left hemisphere (H_L), resulting in a quadrant structure that reflects the anatomical division.

In the global case, all regions are influenced uniformly. In the hemispheric-specific scheme, the matrix is divided into four blocks: intra-hemispheric connections within H_R and H_L are scaled by G_1, while inter-hemispheric connections (between H_R and H_L) are scaled by G_2. This block-wise parameterization allows the model to capture asymmetric integration patterns across hemispheres. Specifically, the long-range term in Eq. (1) is replaced by Eq. (5).

$$G \sum_{\substack{l=1 \\ l \neq k}}^{N} C_{kl}E_l \quad \longrightarrow \quad \sum_{\substack{l=1 \\ l \neq k}}^{N} \left[G_1 \delta_{kl}^{\text{intra}} + G_2 \delta_{kl}^{\text{inter}} \right] C_{kl}E_l, \tag{5}$$

where $\delta_{kl}^{\text{intra}} = 1$ if regions k and l belong to the same hemisphere, and $\delta_{kl}^{\text{inter}} = 1$ otherwise. This extension allows the model to explore the hypothesis that intra-hemispheric and inter-hemispheric coupling are differentially disrupted in schizophrenia. The parameters G_1 and G_2 were systematically varied to assess their impact on the correlation between simulated and empirical functional connectivity, as well as their influence on functional network topology.

2.5   Parameter Values

All simulations were based on the Wilson–Cowan model. The transfer function $S(x)$, defined in Eq. (3), was parameterized with $\mu = 1.0$ and $\sigma = 0.25$, modulating the population response gain. The model included activity-dependent adaptation on the inhibitory-to-excitatory synaptic weight, initialized as $a_{ei}(0) = 2.5$, and evolving according to the excitatory-inhibitory interaction. Other synaptic weights were fixed: $a_{ee} = 3.5$, $a_{ie} = 3.75$, and $a_{ii} = 0$. Refractoriness coefficients were set to $r_e = r_i = 0.5$, with a threshold adaptation term $\rho_E = 0.14$ governing plasticity. Time constants were set to $\tau_e = 10\,\text{ms}$, $\tau_i = 20\,\text{ms}$, and $\tau_\text{p} = 1\text{s}$ for synaptic adaptation. The simulation was integrated using an Euler method with time step $\Delta t_\text{sim} = 1 \times 10^{-4}\,\text{s}$, downsampled to $\Delta t = 1 \times 10^{-3}\,\text{s}$. A transient period of $100\,\text{s}$ was discarded before collecting $100\,\text{s}$ of simulated activity. Gaussian noise was introduced in the excitatory input with standard deviation $\sqrt{D/\Delta t_\text{sim}}$, where $D = 2 \times 10^{-3}$. Empirical structural and functional connectivity matrices, normalized and restricted to 68 cortical regions, were used to couple regional dynamics and evaluate model performance. Each simulation was initialized with $E_0 = I_0 = 0.1$, and unless otherwise specified, a single realization per parameter pair was executed. We performed grid searches over coupling parameters in both models: G in the global coupling scheme, and G_1, G_2 in the hemispheric-specific variant. In all cases, parameters were explored over the range $G \in [0.1, 30.0]$. In the global model, G uniformly scales all long-range excitatory inputs. In the hemispheric-specific model, by contrast, G_1 modulates intra-hemispheric coupling, whereas G_2 controls inter-hemispheric connectivity. Model performance was assessed by comparing the simulated functional connectivity with empirical FC using Pearson correlation and the Euclidean distance between the upper-triangular entries of the respective matrices.

3   Results

We analyze the empirical connectivity matrices for the CTRL and SCHZ groups to highlight their main differences and evaluate how well the simulations reproduce the observed FC patterns. We systematically assess the performance of a whole-brain model based on Wilson–Cowan dynamics. Our analysis is structured around two modeling approaches. First, we consider a single global coupling parameter, G, which uniformly scales the influence of all structural connections across the network. Second, we introduce two distinct coupling parameters: G_1 for intra-hemispheric and G_2 for inter-hemispheric interactions. This parametrization allows us to explore whether differentiating coupling within and between hemispheres improves the model's ability to replicate empirical patterns, particularly in light of known hemispheric asymmetries in schizophrenia. For each configuration, we perform parameter sweeps and compute both the pearson correlation and root mean square error between the simulated and empirical FC matrices. These metrics quantify the model's accuracy and guide the selection of optimal parameters for each group.

3.1   Topological Analysis of Empirical Structural Connectivity

We computed a set of global network metrics on the average SC matrices of the CTRL and SCHZ groups, including clustering coefficient, modularity, average shortest path length, global efficiency, mean strength, and the small-world index. Although minor numerical differences were observed between groups, no consistent or significant trends emerged that would support robust topological distinctions at the global scale. Then we compare SC weighted network histograms between the two groups, as shown in Fig. 2.

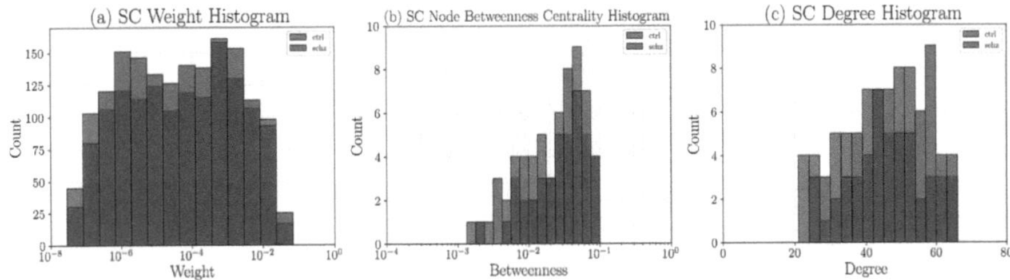

Fig. 2. Comparison of SC weighted network properties between the CTRL and SCHZ groups, based on empirical group-average matrices. Histogram of **(a)** connection weights, **(b)** node betweenness centrality and **(c)** degree distribution. All metrics were computed from the empirical SC matrices restricted to cortical regions.

Figure 2a displays the histogram of SC weights based on group-average matrices. Both groups exhibit a predominance of weak connections, consistent with the known sparsity of long-range anatomical projections. However, the SCHZ group shows a slightly higher count of weaker edges, suggesting a reduction in overall anatomical connectivity strength compared to the CTRL group. In Fig. 2b, the histogram of node betweenness centrality reveals that the CTRL group tends to distribute intermediary structural roles across a broader range of nodes, as indicated by a slightly wider spread in centrality values. In contrast, the SCHZ group exhibits a more concentrated profile, with fewer nodes contributing to long-range communication pathways. Nonetheless, the overall difference between the two groups remains modest at the level of group-average SC. In Fig. 2c, CTRL and SCHZ degree distributions are largely similar, with only subtle shifts, though the SCHZ group appears to exhibit fewer high-degree hubs.

3.2   Wilson–Cowan Model with Uniform Global Coupling G

To investigate the relationship between structural and functional connectivity (SCFC) in both CTRL and SCHZ groups, we simulated the WilsonCowan model on empirical structural connectomes using a single global coupling strength parameter G. We evaluated a range of G values logarithmically distributed from 0.1 to 30.0. For each group and each value of G, we generated 10 simulations, computed the resulting FC matrices, and compared them to the empirical FC using two complementary metrics: the Pearson correlation (r) and the root mean squared error (RMSE).

To illustrate the best-performing simulation under the global coupling model, Fig. 3 presents the results for the SCHZ group with $G = 1.0$. This instance yielded $r = 0.37$ and RMSE $= 0.22$ with respect to the empirical FC. The top row shows the excitatory activity traces in Fig. 3a and the filtered BOLD envelope in Fig. 3b. The bottom row displays the structural connectivity matrix in Fig. 3c, the simulated functional connectivity in Fig. 3d, and the empirical FC in Fig. 3e. The simulated FC captures the overall block organization and inter-hemispheric symmetry observed in the empirical pattern. As observed in Fig. 3d, a noticeable difference appears in the off-diagonal blocks, which are associated with inter-hemispheric connections in the network. The best-performing case for the CTRL group yielded $r = 0.32$ and RMSE $= 0.24$, indicating a slightly worse fit.

Figure 4 shows the average Pearson correlation ($\langle r \rangle$) and the average root mean square error ($\langle \mathrm{RMSE} \rangle$) across simulations as a function of the global coupling parameter G, along with one standard deviation. The CTRL group reached a peak $\langle r \rangle = 0.27 \pm 0.03$, while the SCHZ group achieved a higher maximum of $\langle r \rangle = 0.30 \pm 0.03$, both groups at $G = 1.0$.

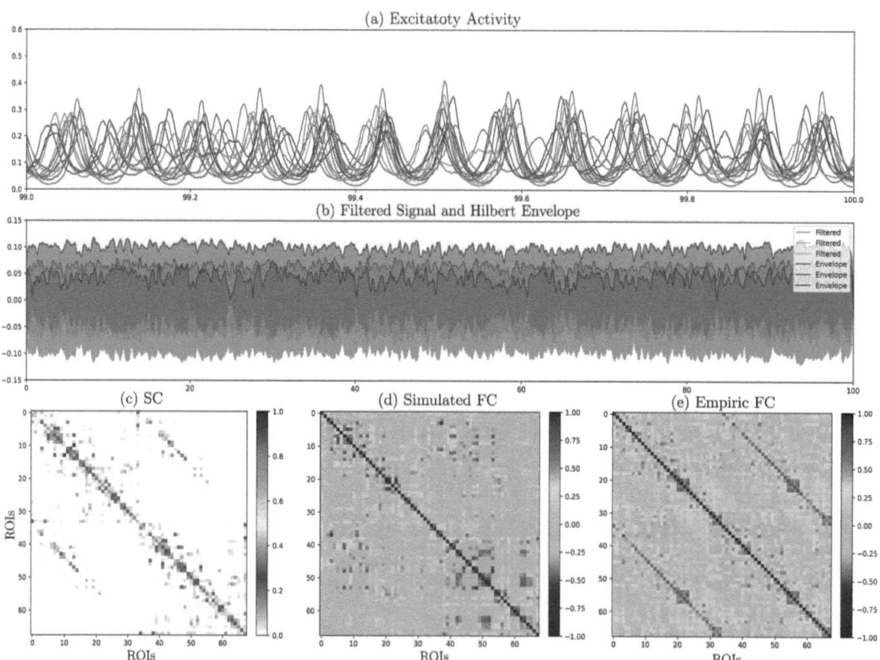

Fig. 3. Group-averaged best-performing simulation for the SCHZ group using global coupling $G = 1.0$. **(a)** Excitatory activity, **(b)** Hilbert envelope, **(c)** SC, **(d)** Simulated FC **(e)** and empirical FC. The simulation yielded $r = 0.37$, RMSE $= 0.22$.

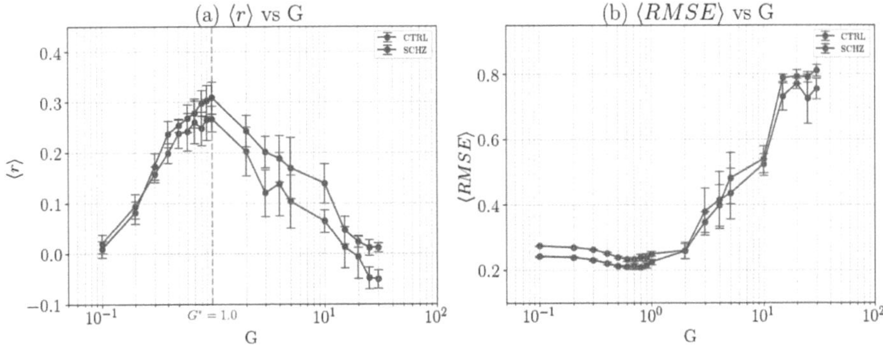

Fig. 4. (a) Average pearson correlation ($\langle r \rangle$) and **(b)** average RMSE ($\langle RMSE \rangle$) between simulated and empirical FC as a function of global coupling strength G, for both CTRL and SCHZ groups. Error bars indicate ± 1 standard deviation across 10 simulations per value of G.

In both cases, the RMSE curve reached its minimum near the same values of G, reinforcing the identification of optimal coupling regimes. Specifically, the lowest RMSE values were $\langle RMSE \rangle = 0.25 \pm 0.01$ for the CTRL group and $\langle RMSE \rangle = 0.20 \pm 0.01$ for the SCHZ group, both groups occurring at $G = 1.0$. On average, the SCHZ group achieved higher correlation values across simulations, suggesting that the model reproduces functional connectivity more accurately in patients than in controls under this global coupling scheme.

3.3 Wilson–Cowan Model with Distinct Coupling Parameters G_1 and G_2

To evaluate whether distinguishing intra-hemispheric and inter-hemispheric interactions improves model performance, we extended the global coupling scheme by introducing two separate parameters: G_1 for intra-hemispheric and G_2 for inter-hemispheric connectivity. To illustrate the best-performing simulation under the hemispheric-specific coupling model, Fig. 5 presents the results for the SCHZ group with $G_1 = 0.80$ and $G_2 = 15.00$.

This configuration yielded a correlation of $r = 0.47$ and RMSE $= 0.20$ when compared to the empirical FC. Figure 5 includes the structural connectivity matrix used for the simulation in Fig. 5a, the resulting simulated FC in Fig. 5b, and the empirical FC used for comparison in Fig. 5c. The simulated FC replicates the modular structure and bilateral symmetry of the empirical matrix, with notable improvements in inter-hemispheric correlations. As observed in Fig. 5b, the enhanced fit is particularly evident in the preservation of off-diagonal block structures, reflecting effective modeling of cross-hemispheric interactions. The best-performing case for the CTRL group yielded $r = 0.40$ and RMSE $= 0.20$ at $G_1 = 1.0$ and $G_2 = 15.0$, indicating a slightly worse fit. On average, the SCHZ group achieved higher correlation values across simulations, suggesting that the

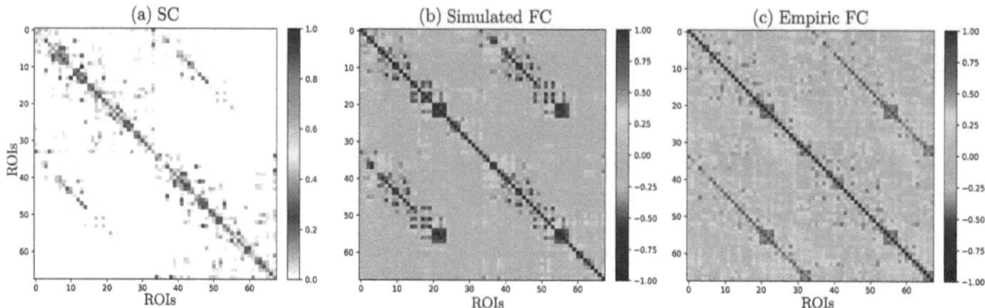

Fig. 5. Group-averaged best-performing simulation for the SCHZ group using hemispheric-specific coupling parameters $G_1 = 0.80$, $G_2 = 15.00$. **(a)** Structural Connectivity (SC) matrix, **(b)** Simulated Functional Connectivity (FC), and **(c)** Empirical FC. The simulation yielded a correlation of $r = 0.47$ and RMSE = 0.20. Panels (a) and (c) correspond to the same subject as in Fig. 3c and Fig. 3e, respectively.

model reproduces functional connectivity more accurately in patients than in controls under the hemispheric-specific coupling scheme.

Figure 6 summarizes the results of a parameter sweep over a wide range of G_1 and G_2 values. Figure 6a,b show $\langle r \rangle$ between simulated and empirical FC for the CTRL and SCHZ groups, respectively. We observe a substantial improvement in performance compared to the uniform coupling case. The optimal configuration for the CTRL group was found at $G_1 = 1.0$, $G_2 = 15.0$, yielding a $\langle r \rangle = 0.36 \pm 0.05$ in Fig. 6a. The SCHZ group achieved an even higher maximum $\langle r \rangle = 0.43 \pm 0.03$ at $G_1 = 0.8$, $G_2 = 15.0$ in Fig. 6b. We observe that, for the CTRL group, the best-performing simulations are located in a more central region of the (G_1, G_2) parameter space compared to the SCHZ group. In the SCHZ case, the region of highest correlation is shifted toward higher G_2 values relative to G_1, indicating a stronger reliance on inter-hemispheric coupling. Moreover, the maximum correlation achieved in the SCHZ group is higher than that of the CTRL group. When comparing the mean correlation peaks, both groups share a same optimal value for G_2, but differ in their optimal G_1. Specifically, the CTRL group requires stronger intra-hemispheric coupling to better replicate empirical FC patterns, whereas the SCHZ group achieves optimal performance with lower G_1. Although not shown, we also computed the RMSE between empirical and simulated connectivity patterns across the same parameter grid. Consistent with the correlation analysis, we found that configurations yielding higher correlations also exhibited lower RMSE values, indicating convergence in both topological correlation and absolute distance.

While the model captures certain qualitative tendencies, such as the correlation between empirical and simulated FC, it does not yet reproduce network metrics comparable to those observed in the empirical data. This suggests that additional refinements are needed to improve the model's ability to replicate the topological organization of functional connectivity.

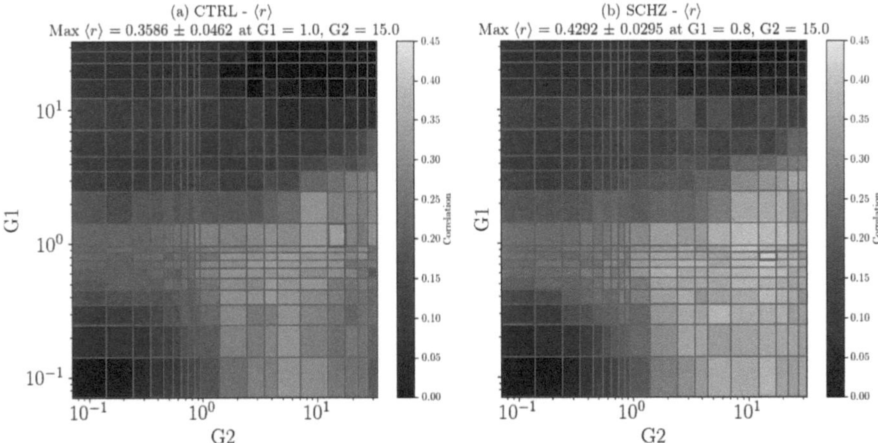

Fig. 6. Parameter sweep across intra-hemispheric and inter-hemispheric coupling strengths G_1 and G_2 in the Wilson–Cowan model. **(a,b)** $\langle r \rangle$ between simulated and empirical FC for the CTRL and SCHZ groups, respectively. The red box in panels (a) and (b) marks the parameter combination that yielded the highest average correlation for each group.

4   Conclusions

In this study, we implemented the Wilson–Cowan model and introduced a hemispheric-specific coupling scheme. We examined both groups and compared structural connectivity network features. In structural connectivity, we found results consistent with previous studies reporting decreased anatomical connectivity strength [9,15], redistribution of central roles across network regions [15], and topological reorganization in schizophrenia [10]. To further explore the mechanistic basis of these alterations, we evaluated the capacity of a biologically grounded neural mass model based on Wilson–Cowan dynamics [1,2,12], in order to reproduce resting-state functional connectivity from empirical cortical structural connectomes in matched control and schizophrenia groups. In our implementation, we differentiated intra-hemispheric and inter-hemispheric anatomical projections via a hemispheric-specific coupling scheme. This modified version systematically outperformed the classic global coupling approach, yielding higher Pearson correlations between simulated and empirical FC across both groups. The improvement was especially pronounced in the schizophrenia group in both models. This may reflect a stronger constraint of functional dynamics by the underlying structural scaffold in schizophrenia, where reduced global integration and increased modularity limit the repertoire of functional configurations. In such conditions, anatomically grounded models may more accurately capture the structurefunction mapping [5,8]. Interestingly, the optimal parameter configuration differed between groups. The SCHZ group achieved a higher maximum correlation of $\langle r \rangle = 0.43 \pm 0.03$ at $G_1 = 0.8$, $G_2 = 15.0$, whereas the

CTRL group reached $\langle r \rangle = 0.36 \pm 0.05$ at $G_1 = 1.0$, $G_2 = 15.0$. Although both groups showed optimal performance in regimes where inter-hemispheric coupling G_2 exceeded intra-hemispheric coupling G_1, the schizophrenia group required a lower G_1 to reproduce empirical FC. This may suggest a diminished role of intra-hemispheric integration in shaping functional dynamics in schizophrenia, potentially reflecting degraded or less functionally effective intra-hemispheric anatomical pathways [15]. Additionally, the SCHZ model displayed good performance across a broader range of G_2 values, indicating a degree of flexibility or compensatory reliance on inter-hemispheric interactions. Together, these findings suggest distinct structurefunction coupling regimes between groups, with schizophrenia exhibiting both reduced intra-hemispheric integration and a more tolerant configuration space for inter-hemispheric coupling. Overall, these findings highlight the value of integrating structural connectivity data with biologically inspired models to gain mechanistic insights into the altered brain dynamics observed in neuropsychiatric disorders.

Data Availability Statement. All simulations were implemented in Python 3.11. The implementation relies on the following open-source libraries: `NumPy 1.26`, `SciPy 1.13`, `pandas 2.2.1`, `matplotlib 3.8.3`, and `Numba 0.60` for just-in-time compilation of performance-critical functions. The Wilson–Cowan model and analysis scripts are structured for modularity and extensibility. The entire simulation pipeline can be reproduced by running the provided main scripts (`run_global.py` and `run_hemispheric.py`). A `requirements.txt` file is provided to facilitate environment replication. The simulation outputs (e.g., empirical and simulated functional connectivity matrices, node activity signals, and computed metrics) are stored in a structured directory under `results/`, which is automatically generated by the code. These outputs include all data used to produce the figures presented in this work. The data that support the findings of this study are openly available in GitHub.

References

1. Wilson, H.R., Cowan, J.D.: Excitatory and inhibitory interactions in localized populations of model neurons. Biophys. J . **12**(1), 1–24 (1972)
2. Wilson, H.R., Cowan, J.D.: A mathematical theory of the functional dynamics of cortical and thalamic nervous tissue. Kybernetik **13**(2), 55–80 (1973)
3. Hagmann, P., et al.: Mapping the structural core of human cerebral cortex. PLoS Biol. **6**(7), e159 (2008)
4. Smith, S.M., et al.: Correspondence of the brain's functional architecture during activation and rest. Proc. Natl. Acad. Sci. **106**(31), 13040–13045 (2009)
5. Deco, G., Jirsa, V.K.: Ongoing cortical activity at rest: criticality, multistability, and ghost attractors. J. Neurosci. **32**(10), 3366–3375 (2012)
6. Daducci, A., et al.: The connectome mapper: an open-source processing pipeline to map connectomes with MRI. PLoS ONE **7**(12), e48121 (2012)
7. Cammoun, L., et al.: Mapping the human connectome at multiple scales with diffusion spectrum MRI. J. Neurosci. Methods **203**(2), 386–397 (2012)
8. Deco, G., Ponce-Alvarez, A., Mantini, D., Romani, G.L., Hagmann, P., Corbetta, M.: Resting-state functional connectivity emerges from structurally and dynamically shaped slow linear fluctuations. J. Neurosci. **33**(27), 11239–11252 (2013)

9. Griffa, A., Baumann, P.S., Thiran, J.-P., Hagmann, P.: Structural connectomics in brain diseases. NeuroImage Clin. **2**, 769–783 (2013)
10. Griffa, A., Baumann, P.S., Thiran, J.-P., Hagmann, P.: Characterizing the connectome in schizophrenia with diffusion spectrum imaging. Hum. Brain Mapp. **36**(1), 354–366 (2015)
11. Griffa, A., et al.: Transient networks of spatio-temporal connectivity map communication pathways in brain functional systems. Neuroimage **155**, 490–502 (2017)
12. Abeysuriya, R.G., et al.: A biophysical model of dynamic balancing of excitation and inhibition in fast oscillatory large-scale networks. PLoS Comput. Biol. **14**(10), e1006007 (2018)
13. Vohryzek, J., et al.: Structural and functional connectomes from 27 schizophrenic patients and 27 matched healthy adults (2020). https://doi.org/10.5281/zenodo.3758534
14. Gutiérrez-Gómez, L., et al.: Stable biomarker identification for predicting schizophrenia in the human connectome. Netw. Neurosci. **4**(3), 521–543 (2020)
15. Guo, S., et al.: Pattern recognition of schizophrenia based on multidimensional spatial feature fusion. Brain-Apparatus Commun. J. Bacomics **2**(1), 2249036 (2023)

Author Index

MIX
Papier aus verantwortungsvollen Quellen
Paper from responsible sources
FSC® C105338

If you have any concerns about our products,
you can contact us on
ProductSafety@springernature.com

In case Publisher is established outside the EU,
the EU authorized representative is:
Springer Nature Customer Service Center GmbH
Europaplatz 3, 69115 Heidelberg, Germany

Printed by Libri Plureos GmbH
in Hamburg, Germany